GW00763776

MATHS

KEY STAGE 1

SCOTTISH LEVELS A-B

ASSESSMENT

JEAN EDWARDS & IAN GARDNER

Published by Scholastic Ltd,
Villiers House,
Clarendon Avenue,
Leamington Spa,
Warwickshire CV32 5PR

Text © 1998 Jean Edwards and Ian Gardner
© 1998 Scholastic Ltd
1 2 3 4 5 6 7 8 9 0   8 9 0 1 2 3 4 5 6 7

Authors
Jean Edwards and Ian Gardner

Editor
Joel Lane

Assistant Editor
Kate Pearce

Series Design
Joy White

Designer
Rachel Warner

Illustration
Ray and Corrine Burrows

Designed using Adobe

British Library Cataloguing-in-Publication Data
A catalogue record for this book is available from the British Library

ISBN 0-590-53640-0

The right of Jean Edwards and Ian Gardner to be
identified as the Author of this Work has
been asserted by them in accordance with the
Copyright, Designs and Patents Act 1988.

CONTENTS

DATA HANDLING 87

SHAPE AND SPACE 107

INTRODUCTION

ABOUT PORTFOLIO ASSESSMENT

Assessment is something that teachers do all the time. It is an integral part of the process of teaching. While much of it goes unrecorded, teachers nevertheless continually formulate judgements based on their observations of children working.

The term 'portfolio assessment' refers to planned interventions that allow the child to demonstrate what he/she knows and can do. Unlike standardised tasks and tests, however, portfolio assessment focuses on qualitative judgements of performance. Although as a teacher you may wish to relate these evaluations to national norms, the objective of such tasks is not to give a percentage, score or grade. The outcomes themselves, recorded by the teacher and/or the child, constitute the evidence. This evidence should not only indicate what the child has achieved, it should also provide pointers as to what knowledge and skills are required for the child to move forward.

The fostering of mathematical capability requires both attention to the way we present the subject and an appreciation that every child learns in a unique way. Portfolio assessment encourages these perspectives by placing the onus on teachers to use professional judgements in presenting and adapting the tasks to suit individual needs. Incorporated as another facet in the practice of teaching, portfolio assessment offers a series of reference points by which to judge the learner. It can also provide valuable feedback to inform future approaches to teaching by highlighting those steps that have proved particularly effective in moving the child's learning forward.

THE CONCEPT OF AN ASSESSMENT PORTFOLIO

Portfolios come in a great variety of formats, and can have different functions for various professions. Compare, for example, the purpose of an artist's portfolio with that of one developed for financial investment. In educational terms, a portfolio is viewed as a window through which we can gain an insight into the individual's developing capability. It is a selection of dated samples of work, illustrating or providing examples of significant performance in a range of contexts and in different areas of a subject. Supported by brief annotations and contextual information from the teacher, the portfolio can provide a measure both of the child's strengths and of those aspects in need of further development.

FUNCTIONS OF THE ASSESSMENT PORTFOLIO

The two main functions of this portfolio are diagnostic and celebratory. In its diagnostic function, the assessment portfolio informs teachers' decisions about the learning environment and about individual children's needs. Assessing what the child knows and how well he/she responds to the experiences presented allows the teacher to make sensitive and informed decisions about future learning steps. By asking probing questions, by closely observing the child's interactions with others, and by analysing recorded outcomes, we can approach a more exact sense of where individual strengths and weaknesses lie.

The diagnostic function

The power of diagnostic assessment lies not in specifying how one child can be judged in relation to another, but in identifying what makes that child's awareness unique. As the teacher gains more information about this awareness, he/she becomes able to fine-tune the teaching to match the needs of the child more precisely. Thus feedback leads to 'feed-forward'; an

ongoing cycle of teaching, assessing and reviewing is established.
Parents may benefit from the diagnostic information you offer them. It is important that such dialogue clearly identifies perceived areas of strength and weakness, and clarifies the mutual responsibilities involved in moving the child's learning forward. In reporting to parents, many schools have found that setting specific goals helps to focus attention on these points.

The celebratory function

The second important function of the assessment portfolio is to document the child's achievements. We should not underestimate the importance of incorporating the learner in this process, as there is arguably no better motivating force than evidence of one's own progress. As teachers, we use this information to gain specific knowledge of the child's stage of development. The detailed evidence, together with earlier samples of work for comparison, can give valuable indications regarding the rate at which progress is being made. The portfolio will enhance the sharing of information in both interviews and written reports.

On a broader front, the portfolio also gives the teacher things to celebrate as groups of children progress over time. In observing their progress, the teacher can identify interventions and teaching programmes which have been particularly effective, and gain a heightened sense of her/his continued professional development.

SCHOLASTIC PORTFOLIO ASSESSMENT AND MATHEMATICAL ASSESSMENT

Assessment in mathematics focuses not only on the child's learned knowledge and skills, but also on the child's ability to apply that learning. Unlike some more formalised approaches to assessment, the portfolio approach aims to be genuinely diagnostic: it highlights particular strengths and misconceptions. This is achieved in many of the activities by presenting tasks which allow for a variety of responses. By opting for a relatively open approach, the teacher is well-placed to identify significant features of an individual's work and to act on that information:

Plan the assessment activity

Conduct the activity and collect information
↓
Review the information gathered
↓
Plan further activity based on the above
↓

The teacher's role in this process is fundamental – both in preparing and managing the learning environment and in taking opportunities to observe, listen, discuss, question, extend and intervene.

Significant assessment possibilities often arise when an unfamiliar problem requires resolution. The activities in *Scholastic Portfolio Assessment* require the child both to draw on their knowledge, skills and understanding and to use and apply them in new ways. This ability to use and apply mathematics lies at the heart of the subject, and is the element that truly means the child is working mathematically.

Towards a whole-school approach

Scholastic Portfolio Assessment lends itself readily to use as the framework for a whole-school approach to maths assessment. Used by the whole school, the activities can provide evidence of continuity and progression across the Reception (P1) and Key Stage 1 (P2 to P4) years. It will be important for a school to make some decisions about which activities are appropriate for each year group, in order to prevent inappropriate repetition. Some activities would be appropriate to repeat in successive years as the child progresses. Teachers could also benefit from sharing pieces of work and reaching a consensus on what the outcomes indicate about a child's achievements.

A portfolio offers benefits for the child and the parent or carer as well. It establishes a dialogue with the child which can be an important early step in active learning. If the child shares in the assessment of her/his progress, he/she gains a broader awareness of expectations and an opportunity to understand what constitutes significant evidence. This can have a motivational benefit, particularly for the child who is anxious or suffers from low self-esteem. Parents also value the opportunity to engage in the learning process. Samples of work constitute a tangible outcome to be shared. An evaluation of such work can lead to a better understanding of the individual's strengths and areas for further development. Portfolio assessment thus has scope for target setting.

In relation to individual pupils, *Scholastic Portfolio Assessment* offers:
- feedback on teaching;
- detailed evidence of progress made over the short and the long term;
- insights into the child's ability to apply her/his learning;
- a bank of evidence to support summative judgements of attainment;
- appraisal of a balance of skills and knowledge;
- insights into the future learning needs of the child.

Used more broadly, it can support a group of teachers in a school by:
- establishing broad judgements of the progress and attainment made by the children in a year group;
- providing feedback on the breadth of curricular provision;
- encouraging a consensus judgement of performance;
- focusing attention on equal opportunity issues in relation to the progress made by different groups;
- drawing attention to the range of teaching and learning styles.

Use and management of the assessment portfolio

The *Scholastic Portfolio Assessment* series covers mathematics, literacy and science. The two mathematics titles offer focused guidance on all areas of the mathematics curriculum. They have been developed to cover relevant parts of the National Curriculum Programmes of Study for England and Wales, the Scottish 5–14 Guidelines and the Northern Ireland Curriculum. They are designed to be used in a flexible way: it is not necessary to follow any specific page order, or to use all of the photocopiable pages. These books give teachers the means to assess key skills and knowledge at whatever times suit their own and the children's needs.

We strongly recommend that the themes presented in this book are integrated into your teaching so that the child comes to each assessment task with some prior experience of the ideas and conventions involved. This then allows a judgement to be made of how well the child is able to apply the experience in a new context. Some of the tasks identify whether skills can be carried through; others confirm the child's understanding.

The resources in this book are aimed at teachers of children at Key Stage 1 (Primary 1–3). A companion volume in this series covers the assessment of mathematics at Key Stage 2 (Primary 4–6). The content coverage in this book consists of four chapters: Number, money and algebra; Handling data; Shape and space; and Measures. Each of these chapters contains:

- **Background information.** This sets out the rationale for the content of the chapter and, in some instances, gives technical advice and background information (for example, on differentiating the assessment of shape from that of number).
- **Teachers' notes.** Although some guidance is detailed on each photocopiable sheet, more comprehensive notes are given here on the conduct and administration of the task. These notes also detail some of the different outcomes that might be expected from children of different ages, abilities and levels of prior experience.
- **Photocopiable assessment sheets.** The left-hand margin of each sheet gives brief notes on the assessment focus, the relevant skills in using and applying mathematics and the nature of the task, along with some assessment pointers. This is convenient for working with the child, and also serves as a reminder at a later date when the portfolio is viewed retrospectively. The remainder of the page presents the activity and acts as a record of the child's work. In some instances, that record will be supported by additions and entries made by the teacher. Many of the sheets are ready to photocopy; others require the addition of a few numbers or words appropriate to the needs of the child.

Use and application of mathematics

You may note from the content coverage outlined above that the child's ability to use and apply mathematics is not detailed within a separate chapter. This important element is integrated throughout the activities. The focus within each activity depends on the nature of the task. In broad terms, the following elements feature: explaining and reasoning; talking about the work; asking and answering questions; selecting materials and mathematics; presenting work in different ways; working in a systematic and organised way; identifying patterns; making predictions; drawing conclusions; and making general statements.

Specific references to using and applying mathematics skills are given on the photocopiable sheets, in the teachers' notes, and in the curriculum charts on pages 15–18 and 173–176. The charts comprise a listing of the book's coverage of the National Curriculum for England and Wales, and links to the Northern Ireland Curriculum and the Scottish 5–14 Guidelines.

When and how to use the assessments

It would be unrealistic to give definite age recommendations for these activities, for several reasons. Firstly, many of the challenges give opportunities for work at various levels of capability, and could justifiably be used two or three times by the same child. A young child, for example, may explore a task at a simple level and record in a way that refers to the objects being handled. With support, there may be scope for discussion, pictorial representation and the opportunity to follow a set of instructions. A child with more experience of the ideas under scrutiny may show greater independence, record symbolically and begin to ask questions of her/his own. An older or able child may make decisions for her/himself and find ways to overcome difficulties encountered along the way. In some cases, the child may begin to make general statements and talk in mathematical terms without ambiguity.

Another reason for not assigning activities by pupil age is that situational factors can have a significant effect on the level of skills and knowledge that a child brings on entry to school. Furthermore, the composition of teaching groups varies widely (sometimes involving a wide age span); and thus it would be unrealistic to expect all the children to undertake the same activities routinely.

Before using the sheets with children, you will need to familiarise yourself with the purpose and conduct of each assessment in order to make any necessary changes to the sheet before photocopying and to gather any additional resources that are required. The sequence in which you use the sheets should be appropriate to the needs of the children. Within each chapter, there are several sections. Within the chapter on 'Number, money and algebra', for example, there is a section dealing with addition. Each section contains what we consider to be a progression of activities, arranged broadly in order of increasing difficulty. This is only a guide, however, and you may well use them in a different order or miss some out altogether. Some activities may be used once and then modified on a future occasion, while others may be inappropriate for your class.

Completed *Scholastic Portfolio Assessment* sheets can be integrated with other ongoing work (from workbooks or folders) to generate a portfolio. Only samples which represent significant or representative achievement should be retained in this way.

The word 'assessment' sometimes conjures up images of a highly formal process. It is important to provide an environment which allays any such anxieties, and to establish work on the portfolio as just another of the classroom routines. In contrast to a typical lesson, however, it is anticipated that the child will be building on skills and ideas that have already been explored on a previous occasion. In some cases, it will be necessary to clarify why the task is being undertaken, and to share the assessment objectives of the task with the child. If the task proves too difficult for the child, it will be appropriate to offer support or to modify the activity. In some circumstances you may even opt to discontinue the task, though this should be avoided if possible as it can lead to a sense of failure. When support is given, it is good practice to annotate or code the child's work to act as a reminder that some additional teaching has taken place. It may be helpful to tell the child what you are writing, in order to maintain openness and mutual trust.

Most teachers will want to select activities which link to work that has taken place recently in the classroom. Before the child begins a task, you should make sure that he/she understands what the task involves. Encourage the child to ask for help if he/she is puzzled. When the child has finished, promote reflection by talking about the work. Offer some immediate constructive feedback so that the child can begin the process of self-evaluation. It is vital that, in doing mathematical work of this nature, the child is not left unhappy or confused. Pupil self-evaluation and teacher evaluation of the activities can be assisted by the use of photocopiable pages 13 and 14.

FURTHER READING

The chapter on Assessment in the Primary Professional Bookshelf title *Teaching Numeracy*, edited by Ruth Merttens (Scholastic, 1997), provides a useful background to the themes discussed in this Introduction.

Record the child's approach to any assessment activity on this sheet

Teacher comments:

Pupil analysis sheet

Length of activity

Short (under 20 minutes) ☐

Medium (20-40 minutes) ☐

Long (over 40 minutes) ☐

Is the activity:

◆ divided up into many short tasks? ☐

◆ divided up into longer, more substantial tasks? ☐

◆ one, holistic task? ☐

Main content objective

Note the PoS statements and AT levels that pupil working within

Number and algebra	Measures	Shape	Handling data

Process objectives (tick as appropriate)

Selection of materials/mathematics ☐

Communication of ideas ☐

Generalising ☐

_____ ☐

_____ ☐

_____ ☐

Other issues (brief comments)

Concentration _____

Independence _____

Understanding _____

Support _____

Any other comments

Teacher's notes, page 12

Mathematics review sheet

Allows self-evaluation by the child of any mathematical activity.

Allow the child time for self-evaluation before discussing his or her responses on the sheet.

Activity content:

Teacher's comments

What did you use?

_____

_____

_____

Who did you work with?

_____

_____

_____

How hard was it?

Easy	OK	A bit hard	Very hard

Did you like it?

NATIONAL CURRICULUM FOR MATHEMATICS (ENGLAND AND WALES)

This grid indicates links between the activities and the relevant sections of the Programme of Study for Mathematics at Key Stage 1. For each activity, reference is made to links with 'Using and applying mathematics' and the appropriate content areas.

cont...

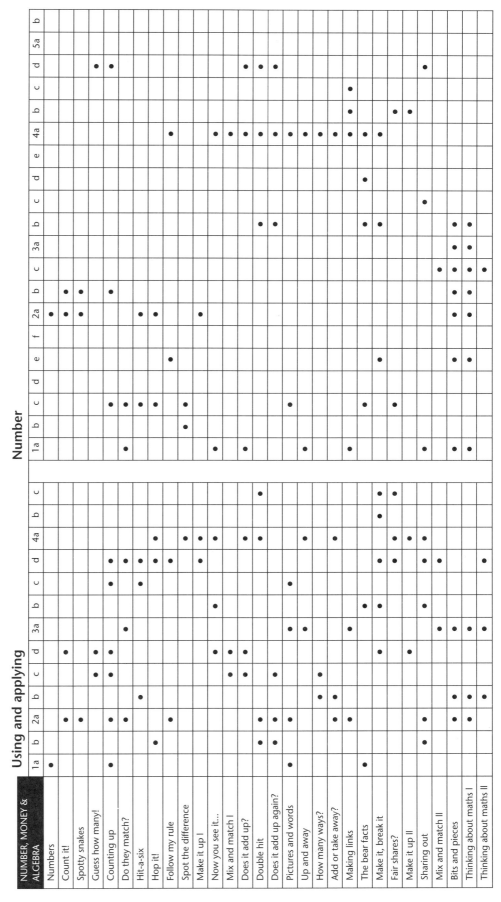

NUMBER, MONEY & ALGEBRA	Using and applying													Number																			
	1a	b	2a	b	c	d	3a	b	c	d	4a	b	c	1a	b	c	d	e	f	2a	b	c	3a	b	c	d	e	4a	b	c	d	5a	b
Numbers	●																			●													
Count it!			●			●														●	●												
Spotty snakes			●																	●	●												
Guess how many!					●	●										●												●					
Counting up	●		●		●	●										●				●													
Do they match?				●											●																		
Hit-a-six																●				●													
Hop it!		●														●				●													
Follow my rule			●												●	●			●									●					
Spot the difference																																	
Make it up I							●							●														● ●					
Now you see it...					●	●								●		●												●					
Mix and match I					●	●		●							●												●					
Does it add up?					●			●						●		●						●						●					
Double hit		●	●	●									●							●			●					●					
Does it add up again?		●	●	●	●			●					●							●			●					●					
Pictures and words	●		●	●	●		●	●						●		●												●					
Up and away										●						●												●					
How many ways?											●			●					●									●					
Add or take away?					●			●			●					●												●					
Making links	●		●	●							●													●			●					
The bear facts	●																						●									
Make it, break it			●			●						●	●									●	●		●			● ●	● ●				
Fair shares?			●							●					●											●		●	● ●				
Make it up II						●		●																									
Sharing out		●	●												●										●			●					
Mix and match II																							●	●	●								
Bits and pieces			●	●			●	●	●	●					●				●		●	●	●	●	●			●					
Thinking about maths I			●	●			●		●						●				●		●	●		●	●								
Thinking about maths II				●			●		●						●								●										

CURRICULUM LINKS CHARTS

Using and Applying

	1a	b	2a	b	c	d	3a	b	c	d	4a	b	c
Before and after	•												
In my head		•					•						
Work it out			•				•				•		
Many times over			•						•		•		
Which comes first?				•		•							
Making numbers					•	•							
Nearest number			•			•		•					
What now?							•						
Shopping	•			•					•				
Target price	•		•						•				
Spend £1	•		•										
Born to shop	•		•	•	•				•				
Fruit corner	•		•	•		•							
In its place	•												
All in order				•	•						•		
Round and round				•	•						•		
Pick a pair								•					•
Up and down			•			•					•		
Number chains				•							•		
DATA HANDLING													
Sorted!		•							•				
Dominoes			•						•		•		
Sisters and brothers		•											
Not this, not that			•						•				
Double sort			•	•									
Sorting tree						•			•		•		
Best of three													
Our favourite colour													
What's the difference?						•					•		
Databases	•		•	•	•	•			•				
Making a graph	•		•	•	•	•			•				

Number

	1a	b	c	d	e	f	2a	b	c	3a	b	c	d	e	4a	b	c	d	5a	b
Before and after	•				•		•													
In my head	•			•	•							•	•		•					
Work it out	•			•	•							•	•		•					
Many times over	•				•						•	•				•	•	•		
Which comes first?								•												
Making numbers				•				•												
Nearest number	•				•	•		•				•	•	•						
What now?								•												
Shopping															•					
Target price			•													•				
Spend £1			•													•				
Born to shop	•										•		•		•	•	•	•		
Fruit corner	•			•										•	•		•	•		
In its place							•													
All in order							•			•					•					
Round and round										•										
Pick a pair							•													
Up and down	•				•							•	•	•	•					
Number chains											•	•								
DATA HANDLING																				
Sorted!																			•	
Dominoes							•												•	
Sisters and brothers																			•	•
Not this, not that																				•
Double sort																			•	•
Sorting tree							•													•
Best of three																				•
Our favourite colour																				•
What's the difference?																				•
Databases	•						•					•			•					•
Making a graph						•	•					•			•					•

cont...

Using and applying | Shape, space and measures

SHAPE & SPACE	1a	1b	2a	2b	2c	2d	3a	3b	3c	3d	4a	4b	4c		1a	1b	c	2a	b	c	3a	b
Flat shapes	●																		●	●		
More 2D shapes							●												●	●		
My first tangram					●										●			●		●		
Short straw, long straw						●			●						●			●	●			
What's my rule?			●			●			●	●								●	●	●		
Is it half?			●							●								●				
3D shape names							●												●	●		
Does it roll? Does it build?	●			●		●			●		●								●	●		
Making boxes	●			●						●									●			
Boxed in					●					●								●	●	●		
Symmetrical or not?				●					●											●		
Mirror image		●				●											●				●	
Fitting together					●	●			●										●	●		
Looking around									●	●	●									●		
What comes next?		●									●	●						●			●	
Where are they?	●						●		●	●					●						●	
Spot the right angles				●		●	●		●	●		●	●									●
Turning						●	●					●	●			●						●
Gaps in the hedge					●	●	●					●	●			●						●
Floor robot				●	●	●				●		●				●		●				●
Hide and seek					●			●	●						●						●	

MEASURING

MEASURING	Using and applying 1a	b	2a	b	c	d	3a	b	c	d	4a	b	c	d	Shape, space and measures 1a	b	c	4a	b
Longer and shorter	•		•				•		•						•			•	•
Hands and feet	•		•						•		•	•			•		•	•	
Taller and shorter				•	•	•			•						•		•	•	•
You and me	•		•						•	•					•		•	•	•
Estimating	•								•					•	•			•	•
Measuring in metres	•			•	•				•						•		•	•	•
Covering up	•				•										•		•		
Heavier and lighter	•		•	•	•	•			•	•	•			•	•		•	•	•
Balancing			•				•		•						•			•	
My mass	•		•						•		•			•				•	•
A kilogram	•		•												•		•	•	•
Measuring with grams						•			•									•	•
Which holds more?						•												•	
Fill the pot							•		•									•	•
More or less than a litre	•			•					•					•	•		•	•	
Measuring with ml				•		•			•						•		•	•	•
Before and after			•	•	•	•			•	•	•			•	•		•	•	
What can we do in one minute?	•		•				•		•						•		•	•	•
Running races	•		•	•		•			•						•		•	•	•
How long are the holidays?	•		•	•					•						•			•	•
Telling the time I	•		•		•	•			•						•		•	•	•
Telling the time II	•			•											•		•	•	
Investigating measures			•																

NUMBER, MONEY AND ALGEBRA

NUMBER, MONEY AND ALGEBRA

This brief introduction outlines significant elements involved in the development of awareness in number, money and algebra through Key Stage 1. In detailing these ideas, it also provides some insight into the content focus of the assessment activities which follow.

NUMBER

Awareness of number

The development of number awareness has many facets which, both before and during the first years of schooling, combine in a period of rapid learning. Most children enter school already knowing the names of some numbers, and they can often recite some of the counting sequence in the correct order. They recognise that numbers have a wide application, and come to realise that unlike a physical item (such as a chair), a particular number can be a property of a set of any objects. In some cases the counting sequence does not always match the physical count (items being missed out or numbers being repeated), and children do not always appreciate that the last number in a count represents the size of the group. Their knowledge and formation of the numerals will also need individual attention.

Larger numbers

Counting beyond the familiar small numbers is also vital for the emergent mathematician. Without hearing the pattern that begins to settle as numbers move beyond 20, the child could be forgiven for believing that our number system is based on a counting sequence where all the numbers are unrelated and each has its own unique sound. A knowledge of our place value structure also helps the child to appreciate that, for example, the calculation of '26 subtract 3' can use the same strategies as the calculation of '6 subtract 3'.

The ability to count on or back from any given number, as well as providing a simple method of calculation, also helps to speed up calculations when work involving partitioning and combining numbers is attempted. Only when the child is confident and secure with these ideas is the introduction of formal methods of recording appropriate. Before this, it is better to encourage the child to use mark-making in ways that relate to her/his mental processes. Through discussion, the teacher may also offer pictorial and symbolic representations which give the child opportunities to reflect on the work covered, to consolidate the learning or to return to it on a future occasion.

Number skills

Alongside the need for knowledge about larger numbers, there is a need to learn basic number facts and to have strategies available for those that are not yet known. An awareness that addition and subtraction are interrelated helps the child to make sense of situations, especially when the approach to a task is not prescribed or is unclear.

It is important to make practical number apparatus available to the child, and at the same time to continue to refine and extend mental approaches.

The latter can be developed, to a large extent, through talking to the child and raising awareness of the strategies he/she has employed and others he/she might have used.

Ordering

Ordering is a skill which is implicit in learning the counting sequence. At a higher level, it requires a knowledge of the decade order and a broader understanding of the base ten nature of our number system.

Fractions

Work on fractions is also introduced at Key Stage 1. The child's awareness of fractions is often developed through work on partitioning where the essential feature is that, in order to be equivalent, fractional quantities must be the same proportion of the whole from which they were derived. By exploring this concept in a range of contexts, including areas beyond the remit of this chapter, the child begins to make sense of common fractions. (The activities in Chapter 3, 'Shape and space', offer some appropriate spacial contexts for exploring fractions as parts of a whole.)

MONEY

Background experience

The child's pre-school experience of money will depend on the extent to which he/she has had opportunities to handle and 'use' it. If the child has not had real contexts for handling money, then he/she may be unaware of its purpose and importance. Furthermore, the fact that coins come in a great range of denominations can be quite confusing for a child who has been taught that 1 always stands for one object.

Real and symbolic values

Within the topic of money, the notion of **conservation** is important. Seeing how an amount of money can be represented in several different ways by re-ordering coins or exchanging some for others, the child comes to a clearer understanding of this principle. As her/his confidence in handling money develops, so too does the child's ability to use sums of money up to and beyond a pound. The introduction of decimal notation as a convention in recording facts about money offers the child an early introduction to decimal fractions.

ALGEBRA: PATTERN

Mathematical patterns

An important strand running alongside that of the number system is that of patterns and relationships. Counting in twos is an activity which engages the young child and which leads, depending on the starting point, either to the odd or to the even counting sequence. Repeating number patterns can be appealing to the child, not least because they build on earlier experiences involving colour patterns. Such patterns become overtly mathematical when we identify their ordinal significance, or when we replace variables of colour with those of number, orientation, size and shape.

Number facts

Work on pattern also serves to reinforce other work in number. By developing an organised approach to finding number bonds to ten, for example, the child can be confident of finding all the possible combinations. Secondly, counting in steps other than one develops sequences which are later formalised into knowledge of multiplication facts. An awareness of how these facts are generated helps to fill in the gaps in the child's existing repertoire of instant recall.

TEACHING NOTES FOR INDIVIDUAL ACTIVITIES

Number

Numbers

page 38

Counting forwards and backwards This sheet is appropriate for use alongside many routine counting activities, to reinforce and assess counting skills. Choose the context for this assessment task. You might use a classroom context such as counting photos of children, biscuits for snack time, toy animals, cars, shells in the sand tray or parts of a construction kit. The assessment sheet should be filled in with the child, allowing the child to record in her/his own way where appropriate and noting the child's comments on the sheet alongside.

The first part of the sheet will allow you to assess the child's awareness of numbers in her/his own daily life and any emergent recording he/she is able to attempt. You might initiate the talk with questions about the child's house number, age, and so on.

The second and third parts of the sheet allow you to assess how far the child can count orally, and which number symbols the child can record. Both of these tasks will allow you to go as far as is appropriate with the individual child. Some children might be working with the numbers 1 to 3 while others might go on to 20 and beyond, depending on their previous experiences with counting and number symbols. Figure 1 shows a possible answer to the second task. Not all children will start counting at 0. You might prompt the child by asking her/him to think of the smallest number he/she can.

Figure 1

I counted <u>animals</u>
There were <u>6</u>

I counted <u>shells</u>
There were <u>10</u>

Count it!

page 39

Counting/writing numbers Before the task, decide on the range of numbers to be assessed (from 10 to 25, 10 to 50 or 50 to 100). Collect some small objects to be counted and group them together in pots, saucers or bags. You can set the task in the context of topic work by using relevant objects such as seeds, plastic dinosaurs or shells. The teacher should also provide appropriate apparatus that the child may choose to use, such as paper, pencils, number lines and pots.

While the children are working on the first part of the task, ask each individual child to count orally. Suggest places to start and stop – for example, counting on from 50 to 70 or back from 80 to 63. This will also give you the opportunity to ask the child how he/she counted his/her collections. Strategies might include grouping the objects in 2s or 10s, making notes or keeping a running total. Ideas such as these might come from an initial discussion about ways to make counting easier. You can also note the child's accuracy in counting objects and in counting orally.

Spotty snakes

page 40

Counting Drawing spots on the snakes for the child to count should enable you to match the difficulty of the sheet to the individual. Some children's snakes might have between 0 and 5 spots, others might go up to 20.

If the child's ability to *count* is the important element of this assessment, you might wish to provide number lines or stick-on numbers for the child's recording. Alternatively, you may prefer the child to try to write the numeral from memory if assessment of this knowledge is intended.

Guess how many!
page 41

Estimating This assessment may be set in the context of ongoing work in the classroom. For example, the child could estimate the number of toy animals, biscuits, play people or Lego bricks. Decide in advance on the size of numbers to be estimated. Younger children might work with numbers between 5 and 20, and older or more confident children might try numbers to 30. Before the children work on the sheet, remind them about estimating. An estimate can be explained as a 'sensible' or 'thoughtful' guess which is quite close to the actual number.

Tell the children about the range the numbers fall within (see above), so they are aware of the smallest and largest numbers that could occur. This will help to focus their estimating. Draw shapes/objects on the worksheet for the child to estimate.

After the task, talk to the child about how close her/his estimates were. Can the child make a sensible estimate? The closeness of the estimate might depend on the size of numbers being used. What strategies does the child use when estimating? (If he/she has none, this might result in wild guesses.) Appropriate strategies might include saying 'more than 10' or 'less than 10', 'nearer 10 than 20' or 'nearer 20 than 10', and so on.

Counting up
page 42

Counting with larger numbers You will need a large collection of seeds or dried pulses and some pots (such as paper cups). Decide how to pair the children for the assessment: you might consider pairing children of similar ability, children who work productively together or children of different ability (for support). Decide how long they will have to work on the task. Each child will need a copy of the sheet to record on. You may scribe for the child where appropriate.

During the task, ask each pair how they arrived at their estimate. Before they find out how many seeds there are, you may wish to share suggestions about ways of doing this; or you may wish to leave it completely open. At this point, ask the children to record their partner's name, their initial estimate and their intended methods on the first part of the sheet.

When they have had about half the time available to them stop them, and ask each pair to tell you how they are getting on. If they are struggling to find a strategy or to co-operate, offer guidance. In particular, ask them whether they think their initial estimate was sensible. When you have decided the time is up, ask the children to record their results.

Look for the following assessment points:
• Do the children devise a useful method and use it consistently? (For example: tallying to keep track of the count; dividing up the counting task and then adding the results back together; grouping in consistent sets such as 10s, 20s or 100s.)

• Do they modify their method if necessary? (For example, if it is taking too long.)
• Do they work co-operatively? (For example, by dividing the task up and sharing the counting or grouping.)
• Can they revise their estimate after working for a while, having learned more about what they are dealing with?
• Can they describe and justify what they are doing, in particular the maths they have used?

Do they match?

page 43

Matching one to one You may prefer the child to pair up some real objects and then use the assessment sheet to record the activity. The sheet could be completed by the child or used as a recording proforma by the teacher. Introduce, if necessary, the idea of pairing objects to identify whether two

sets of objects are equal in number. Use the word 'more' when discussing the need for an extra object.

A space is provided in each section for the child to record pictorially the additional item that is required. Alternatively, you could instruct the child to record in words, for example: 'I need one more cup.' An older or more able child might be introduced to the terms 'fewer' and 'less' and use these when comparing the two sets (for example, 'I need one less saucer').

Hit-a-six

page 44

Matching numerals (1–6) to a quantity Give each child a copy of the sheet. Explain that there are two game boards on the sheet to allow them to play this game twice. Go through the rules on the sheet. Though some groups may be able to play the game without your intervention, you will need to observe and question individuals at some point to establish whether the assessment points have been fulfilled. In particular, you should identify whether, for example, a child who has entered a score of 2 on a previously empty strip can count on from this to discover what score is needed to complete that line. A more able child should begin to show an awareness of strategic play by having several different options available to increase the probability of making a move on her/his turn.

Hop it!

page 45

Counting on from one number to another Choose a target number which is appropriate to the individual or group. Demonstrate how to complete a line on the table by starting with a number near the left-hand end of the number line. Enter this number in the first column to indicate a 'start' number. Now 'hop' along the number line in jumps of one, counting how many jumps it is to the target number. Enter this in the second column. Ask the child to complete the rest of the table by selecting her/his own start numbers.

Use the assessment checklist on the sheet as pointers. Make sure that the child is counting on correctly and not including the start number in the count. Children who find this task relatively easy can be asked to count between given start and finish numbers without making use of a number line for support. Record successful attempts as comments at the foot of the page (for example, 'Can count on within 20 without using the number line'). Establish whether a more able child recognises the link between the third column and the sum of the two numbers in the first and second columns.

Follow my rule

page 46

Matching numbers according to a given rule When preparing the sheet for use, make sure that each number in the left-hand column is paired with a number in the right-hand column. Some possible connecting rules are: 'is half of'; 'is 2 less than'; 'add to make 20'; 'is 3 times'.

The older or more able child will be able to combine larger numbers and/or apply more complex rules. A younger or less able child will find a rule such as 'this number comes before' suitably challenging. A task which involves addition or subtraction may be more appropriate to a child with some understanding of basic computation, whereas a rule using multiplication will be suitable only if multiplication has already been introduced in other practical contexts.

Provide items to aid calculation if necessary (for example, cubes or calculators). Explain the mathematics that governs the connecting line on the diagram, then ask the child to join other pairs of numbers which satisfy the same rule.

Use the assessment checklist given on the sheet as pointers. In particular, you should assess how the child calculates the pairings, and whether the task is completed without practical materials.

Spot the difference

page 47

Number bonds to 6 You will need enough small counters to allow each child to work with their set number. Six counters each is suggested as a suitable introductory number.

Ask the child to record her/his work in the space below the domino drawing. At this stage, you could be unspecific about the style of the recording.

The reference to conservation on the assessment sheet relates to the need for the child to appreciate that the number of spots remains the same regardless of the way it is partitioned.

A younger or less able child may adopt a pictorial style of recording, and may only find some of the possible combinations. An older or more able child may systematically work out all the combinations and represent each one symbolically as a conventional addition sum such as $2 + 4 = 6$. The child's explanation at the foot of the page may also be soundly based on an awareness of number patterns.

Make it up I

page 48

Representing a given number in several ways With groups of children, it may be prudent to provide different target numbers to prevent copying and to match the target numbers to individual needs (judged from prior attainment and experience). Some children will be able to record their answers as calculations (for example, $12 - 9$), whereas others may simply represent a target of 3 as three eggs, three fish, and so on.

Use any opportunities to talk to the child about the task and try to look for examples of finding number facts by using a generating sequence (for example, $10 - 2$, $11 - 3$, $12 - 4...$). Some able children may even recognise that 'the sums could go on forever'. Using a generating sequence would indicate an understanding of number facts and an ability to organise them instead of working randomly; however, a child who only uses a single generating sequence to find examples is playing safe and may lack confidence. In order to assess capability fully, it may be necessary to ask the child whether he/she can use fractions and/or different types of operation (such as multiplication). A younger or less able child may find just a couple of solutions, each one being generated in a random manner.

Now you see it...

page 49

Use of complementary addition You will need a sheet of card (to use as a screen) and a set of cubes or counters. Six counters will make a suitable set for a child who is unfamiliar with this task.

Follow the instructions for this activity given on the assessment sheet. The 'check' boxes below the 'guess' boxes allow the child to record the actual solutions, and allow you to assess the accuracy of the predictions. The term 'complementary addition' on the sheet refers to the skill of identifying a number which 'makes up' another number to a required total.

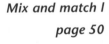

The accuracy of the child's predictions, together with your observations, will provide some evidence of her/his ability in this area. You should ask the child how he/she 'knew' the answers. An able child might typically relate the task to a subtraction or addition problem, using her/his knowledge to calculate the appropriate answer rapidly. A child at an earlier developmental stage with computation may take longer to present an answer, and may attempt to visualise the required number by counting her/his cubes and then counting on from that. Such a child may find it difficult to explain how the prediction was arrived at.

Mix and match I

page 50

Early addition Write numbers in the three circles and six squares at the edge of the activity sheet. The numbers in the three circles must represent the totals of the three pairs of numbers in the squares. For example, a possible set might be: 3, 4, 4, 5, 5, 6 in the squares and 8, 9, 10 in the circles. In this example, there is more than one correct arrangement; where appropriate, you may wish to point this out to the child.

To some extent, your assessment will be based on the size of the numbers the child is dealing with. The more able child, for example, will be able to handle numbers that give totals to 20 and beyond. In some cases, it may be necessary to simplify the task by using four squares and two circles. The assessment checklist on the sheet can be used to note the child's approach to the task.

Does it add up?

page 51

Triple addition bonds Prepare the sheet by selecting an appropriate sequence of consecutive numbers. The most basic set is 1 to 5. Possible alternatives include:
- 0, 1, 2, 3, 4
- 2, 4, 6, 8, 10
- 10, 11, 12, 13, 14

These sets represent a progression in difficulty. The most able child may identify a significance in the first, third and fifth numbers of these sequences (see below).

NB The arrangements can differ quite significantly, because the consecutive nature of the sequence allows three different numbers (the first, middle and last) to be placed in the central square. Less significant differences can arise from rotating a successful arrangement.

The younger or less able child may trial combinations in a random manner. The older or more able child may apply logic in 'balancing' the numbers, and use trial and improvement. He/she may also be able to explain how the solutions were found. Challenge the most able children further by moving on to 'Does it add up again?' on page 53.

Double hit

page 52

Using an addition grid Prepare the sheet for individuals or groups by entering an identical pair of totals (for example, 7 and 9) in each of the seven rectangles. It is important that the child is familiar with the conventions of an addition grid.

Work through the first grid together, explaining that the two numbers provided on each grid represent the target totals. Point out that, although all the answers on the page are the same, there are lots of different ways of making these totals. Start by placing a number (for example, 3) in the far left-hand circle. Ask the child what numbers would need to be added to that number to make the target totals (in this example, 4 and 5). Enter these numbers in the two circles above the squares to complete the addition grid. Now tell the child that he/she must find six different ways of completing the grids, recording them on the sheet.

+	4	6
3	7	9

Listen and talk to the children to establish the strategies he/she uses to find suitable combinations – for example, making the number underneath the addition sign one more than on the previous grid and adapting the top numbers accordingly. Occasionally, you may even be asked whether numbers less than 0 are allowed. A young or less able child may find the layout of the addition grid problematic in itself, and may only find one or two correct examples. Such a child is unlikely to see the interrelatedness of the numbers in the grid.

Does it add up again?

page 53

Addition involving several numbers This task is similar to, but provides more challenge than, the task on page 51. Encourage the child to see that there is more than one possible solution, and to record successful attempts on the small crosses. He/she should go on to list all the possible solutions.

Note how the child adds five numbers together – for example, by adding on each number in the order they are arranged, or by using other strategies (such as adding the numbers and then arranging them). An able child may use a knowledge of number patterns by, for example, placing bonds of 10 at opposite ends of the arms.

Pictures and words

page 54

Contextualising a number sentence in words or pictures Prepare numerical problems at a level which is suitable for the child. Decide whether to focus on word stories or on pictures, or to allow either form of presentation.

This task identifies the extent to which a child can 'model' a numerical problem. For example:

I had 5p. My mum gave me 3p, so I had 8p altogether.

Assessment of the child's work will depend on the relative difficulty of the questions set:
- Initial level – addition/subtraction.
- Middle level – multiplication.
- Upper level – division.

Up and away
page 55

Partitioning a set between three subsets and recording the results
Provide each child with a copy of the activity sheet. Alternatively, you may prefer to make a reusable version (laminated on card) and use photocopies for recording as the child progresses through the task. A suitable number of cubes or counters for the child to work with might be 10.

Demonstrate how the cubes might be distributed between three balloons. Ask the child how the results could be recorded (or specify a way of doing this.) Some children might be able to record the arrangement as an addition sum (for example, $2 + 3 + 5 = 10$). There is space outside the balloons to record some answers, though the child may need to continue on another sheet.

This task allows assessment of capability in working with larger or smaller numbers (through differentiation by task). Observe the child to establish whether answers are being generated randomly or systematically. For example, an older or more able child may create a new combination by moving just one cube from one balloon to another. Such a child may also appreciate the scale of the task of finding all possible combinations. A younger or less able child may be more comfortable working with just two balloons, and may offer only a few solutions which are randomly generated. In such cases, some of the solutions may be inaccurate. If appropriate, 'Spot the difference' (page 47) could be used as a support activity.

How many ways?
page 56

Adding two 2-digit numbers and arranging the digits to find the largest/smallest total A suitable introductory set of number cards would be 1, 2, 3, 4, though some children could work with larger numbers. The children will need to be familiar with vertical addition involving tens and units. If horizontal addition is preferred, the sheet will require modification.

If necessary, demonstrate initially how to make a total by arranging the cards on the grid and adding the tens and units. When the child is doing the task, remind her/him to find all the combinations. An able child could work with an arrangement which involves totals greater than 100.

This task will give you some indication of whether the child understands place value. It requires an awareness of the conventions of vertical addition. An able child may work systematically and succeed in finding all the possible combinations with four digits. If the child is comfortable with decade order, he/she should be able readily to identify the largest and smallest totals.

Add or take away?
page 57

Identifying + or – operations and recognising patterns If the child decides to use cubes or a number line, this should be recorded on the sheet. After the child has completed the task, he/she should be given the opportunity to describe how he/she worked out the answers and whether he/she noticed anything while doing the task. Scribe any interesting comments.

This task will give you the opportunity to assess the following:
- Can the child identify the correct sign?
- Does the child need/want to use apparatus to check?
- Can the child tell you about any pattern or generalised finding? Some children might spot that if the answer is bigger than the two initial numbers,

the number sentence must be an 'add'; whereas if the answer is smaller than the first number, the number sentence must be a 'take away'.

Making links
page 58

Selecting different number operations Choose numerals for the boxes suitable to the ability level of the individual child or group. Explain how the connection line indicates that the two numbers are to be added, subtracted ('find the difference') and/or multiplied. Explain that any box can be connected to any other, and that these combinations should be recorded (in the larger box underneath the diagram) in the form of a sum (for example, 4 – 2 = 2). You may prefer to limit the choice of operations available to the child. The task allows for a vast number of connections to be made, and it is expected that the child will only sample some of the possibilities. Encourage the child to make a record of each link as he/she progresses through the task.

A younger or less able child may choose (or be directed) to restrict the scope to addition only. If this is the case, you should identify how solutions are arrived at and whether, for example, counting materials are required. The more able child will probably use a wide range of operations and will readily identify the number combinations and operations which lead to the largest and smallest answers.

At this stage, you might also question the child to confirm that he/she understands what multiplication means in terms of repeated addition and/or multiples of sets. In making a judgement of the child's ability to use different number operations, you should evaluate the accuracy with which each type of calculation is carried out.

The bear facts
page 59

Subtraction as 'taking away' You will need a set of small number cards with a range up to the number of bears that the child will be working with. For most children, working to and within 10 will be adequate. If a child is competent at dealing with subtraction beyond this number at a mental level, it is unlikely that this task will sufficiently engage him/her. Plastic bears or other characters may be used instead of cut-outs, though the latter should be used for the child to paste down a number story at the end.

The task should be carried out using the picnic mat consistently as a model, with the child physically moving bears and placing appropriate number cards in the second and third boxes (establishing the number to enter in the third box by counting the number of bears left on the mat). When the child has recorded the full number sentence in written form, ask her/him to make up some more bear stories using some or all of the characters.

Less confident children will need support throughout this task. Able pupils may notice some patterns in their answers – for example: 10 – 4 is 6 and 10 – 6 is 4, the numbers are just 'swapped around'; if you add the last two numbers, they make the first number. You could make up a related story to see whether the child can visualise the problem and give an answer without having to use the characters. Note any significant comments and/or observations, using the assessment checklist on the sheet as a guide.

Make it, break it
page 60

Calculate differences between numbers and recognise patterns Although the sheet features 10 interlocking cubes, any suitable number can be used. Make sure that the initial example has been clearly understood by the child before asking her/him to explore different examples. You may choose to specify the method of recording (for example, pictorial or symbolic), or to leave it open for further assessment.

Able children may notice that for a set of 10 cubes, odd differences cannot be found. In such cases, different stick lengths could be investigated to see whether this applies to other even numbers. Less able children will find the numerical and recording demands of this task sufficiently challenging. If the child cannot calculate the differences, the task is too difficult for her/him. In such cases, a smaller number of cubes should be selected for the child to break into as many two-part combinations as possible.

The child's own recording and the assessment checklist, along with any annotated evidence you gather, should provide a strong insight into her/his ability to calculate differences and to identify patterns.

Fair shares?
page 61

Partitioning into subsets The number of cubes which the child will need will depend on the numbers he/she is given to work with. You should provide additional numbers (in the lower boxes) at a level that will sufficiently challenge the individual child.

The younger or less able child may not appreciate that each of the subsets must be equal in size. The older or more able child will often work out a pattern to help her/him predict results:
• 'If it is odd, it won't share.' (two subsets)
• 'It will share if it is in the 3 times table.' (three subsets)

Make it up II
page 62

Half and quarter of a whole This activity is principally an individual task, although you can add dice to provide a game for 2–4 players (see below). Essentially, this activity deals with conservation: a whole unit may be represented in several different ways. It is important to talk to the child to see whether the activity has been conducted with understanding. You will need to make sure that the child appreciates that a cut-out half section represents a half of one circle.

This sheet can also be used for a game with a dice labelled $0, 0, \frac{1}{4}, \frac{1}{4}, \frac{1}{2}, \frac{1}{2}$. The players take turns to roll the dice and pick up the fraction indicated by the outcome. This piece can be added to any one of the circles on the player's sheet. The winner is the first player to completely fill all three of her/his circles.

Note that the assessment focuses on the language used as well as the practical aspects of combining fractions in different ways. A younger or less able child may manage the task but have insufficient mathematical vocabulary to explain her/his work. An older or more able child will recognise the equivalence of fractions and will be capable of answering direct questions of the type 'How many quarters make a whole?' He/she will work logically through the task of finding three different combinations, and could go on to working with an extended set of fractions including eighths.

Sharing out
page 63

Sorting into equal subsets You might wish to set this task in a context by using small objects linked to a current unit of work, such as shells or seeds. Observing this task can give you an insight into the child's method of exploring possible arrangements. Some children might group at random, often choosing numbers that will not result in equal sets. Others might use their recall of multiplication facts to work in a more efficient manner.

When the child is recording, he/she will use pictures, writing or calculations as directed. If the child does not readily use the division sign, you may wish to prompt her/him by showing how the sign is used and asking her/him to try recording combinations in that way. You may feel this to be inappropriate for some children, if they are finding the task of sharing difficult or confusing. Children who understand multiplication and division thoroughly could be challenged further by giving them a larger number to work with on the back of the sheet.

Mix and match II
page 64

Solving problems involving multiplication and division The child must be familiar with the conventional symbols for × and ÷. If the child lacks confidence or mental agility, you may elect to provide appropriate counting apparatus. The task is closed, since the numbers are prepared in advance of photocopying. Discussion with the child will identify how well the interrelatedness of multiplication and division is understood.

Your assessment should differentiate the extent of understanding in the following ways:
- the degree of support required;
- the use of apparatus;
- the quality of mathematical language used;
- the amount of trial and improvement required.

At Key Stage 1, the child will typically be introduced to formal division at a relatively late point. Inability to record using the division sign or to recall division facts will thus not be unusual.

Bits and pieces
page 65

Half and quarter of a quantity You will need to prepare two dice labelled as indicated on the sheet. You may prefer children to fill in the sheet individually or as a collaborative task in pairs. Game instructions are given on the sheet.

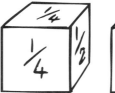

While the group is working through the task, you should try to listen to the conversations in order to ascertain the methods being used to work out scores. If this is not clear, you may need to question individuals about the strategies they have employed (for example, 'How did you find a quarter of 8?'). A confident or able child could then be asked similar questions which go beyond the range of this task (for example, 'What is a quarter of 20? How did you work it out?').

Thinking about maths I and II
pages 66 and 67

These two tasks assess the child's ability to respond independently to oral questions. They cover a range of number skills and concepts. The child should be encouraged to use apparatus to help with working out. Take care to allocate a suitable amount of time for the task; this is not a timed assessment, but inability to find a reasonably quick method should be noted.

Questions for Sheet 1
1. Tick the set which contains 5 stars.
2. Tick the set which contains 8 circles.
3. Draw 10 crosses in the box.
4. Write the number that comes after 8.
5. Write the number that comes before 7.
6. Which is the biggest number, 4 or 6?
7. Which is the smallest number, 3 or 5?
8. If you had 3 felt-tipped pens and your friend gave you 2 more, how many would you have altogether?
9. If you had 7 marbles and you gave 4 to your friend, how many would you have left?
10. What comes next in this pattern, 32132132?

Questions for Sheet 2
1. Tick the set which contains 14 counters.
2. What is 4 + 5?
3. What is 8 – 3?
4. Write these numbers: 22, 32, 13, 31. Put a circle round the biggest number.
5. Write these numbers: 48, 14, 28, 84. Put a circle round the biggest one.
6. What is half of 12?
7. Write three odd numbers that you know.
8. If you had 5 felt-tipped pens and your friend gave you 6 more, how many would you have altogether? Write the number sentence.
9. If you had 12 felt-tipped pens and you gave 4 to your friend, how many would you have left? Write the number sentence.
10. Tick the set that contains 43.

When you talk with the child about her/his answers, you might use the child's mistakes to set new targets or to demonstrate the importance of careful recording. For example, children often do not realise how important it is to write the digits of a number in a certain order until they link it to someone else reading the number differently from the way they intended (for example, someone reading the number twelve as twenty-one because it has been written in digits as 21).

Before and after, In my head, Work it out, Many times over
pages 68–71

Using mental methods of computation These assessments of mental methods have been left open-ended to allow you to decide the range of numbers and operations to be used. The structure and the general assessment focus are provided for each task on the photocopiable pages. The expectation is for the children to work mentally, not using equipment. If the child is at the stage of needing apparatus, he/she is not ready to be assessed in this way. The other important aspect of these assessments is that the children are given opportunities to explain what they are doing; this will give you a valuable insight into their mathematical thinking. These assessments can be carried out by a group. If children find taking turns difficult, it would be advisable to assess them individually.

Before and after
page 68

When asking the questions, you should use language the child will be familiar with – for example, 'more than, less than... more than, fewer than... the number before, the number after...' Structure a range of numbers to work with, such as 0 to 5, 0 to 20 or 0 to 50. You can adapt this as you are working to extend children who are working confidently.

Note the child's responses to your questions; in this assessment you are focusing on mental operations, not the ability to record. The child's drawing of her/his mental images of the numbers will help you to suggest ways of organising number facts mentally. The child's drawing of her/his mental image of the number line may give a valuable indication of the range he/she feels confident with using mentally. You should note whether the child responds to the mathematical language used; whether the child answers instantly or with some thought; and whether the child can respond to a variety of questions and perhaps generalise about them (for example, 'More than is like adding, the numbers are always bigger.')

In my head
page 69

Your questions can use either addition or subtraction, or a mixture. As before, you can alter the range and demand of the calculations as you go along. Decide initially on a range of numbers to work with – for example, within 10, between 10 and 20 or from 0 to 20. You could also set the task in a context if you wish, perhaps by linking the questions to things in the classroom such as pencils, rubbers, books or toys.

NUMBER, MONEY & ALGEBRA

You should note the child's answers on the sheet, since the emphasis here is on mental methods rather than on recording (unless you feel that the child can record quickly and easily). You should also note the accuracy of the child's answers. If he/she uses any visible signs of working, you should note these down. Children sometimes use their fingers or move their heads as they count on an internal number line. The child's final drawing of how he/she visualised one of the calculations will help to illustrate her/his mental methods. Ask the child to explain these methods and note her/his comments in the 'What I did' thought bubble alongside the child's own drawing or writing.

Work it out!
page 70

Decide beforehand on the series of operations that you will ask for. The number and difficulty of the operations should depend on what you know about the child's ability.

Some possible challenges are as follows:
• **Addition and subtraction to 20:** Start at 10. Add 5. Take away 7. Take away 3. Add 9.
• **Using pattern and place value:** Start at 4. Add 10. Add 2. Take away 10. Add 20.
• **Using 2-digit numbers:** Start at 40. Take away 20. Add 5. Add 20. Add 40.

During the activity, you should note any obvious methods the child uses. The child's final drawing and explanation of how he/she worked out one of the challenges will be useful for assessment of this. Some children may be using and applying their knowledge of number bonds and patterns effectively. Other children may be working by counting on and back, which with larger numbers is far more time-consuming.

Many times over
page 71

The first part of the task should be completed individually. If the child is able to recall multiplication facts for 2, 5 and 10 times tables effectively, proceed to the second part of the task. Devise a series of questions which include using multiplication facts mentally – for example:
• Start with 2. Multiply by 2. Multiply by 10.
• Start with 4. Multiply by 2. Multiply by 5.

During the activity, you should note any obvious methods the child uses – for example, counting on in equal steps rather than instant recall of number facts. The child's final explanation of her/his methods will be useful for assessment. A child who has understood the number facts thoroughly will be able to use the knowledge that two eights are 16 to predict that eight twos will also be 16. Some children may employ halving/doubling and adding strategies, for example: 4×5 is double 2×5; 7×10 is 2×10 plus 5×10.

Which comes first?
page 72

Ordering numbers Prepare sets of five numbers within the range being assessed. For this task, the apparatus used could be number tiles, number cards or pieces from a number jigsaw. With younger children, scribe from the child's arrangement (if the ability to record is not being assessed). Look for indications of whether the child can: order numbers within the given range; record the numbers accurately; insert numbers into a sequence; work methodically to complete the task.

This task can be structured to fit a range of ability levels through the choice of numbers – for example, numbers to 10, to 20, to 100 or to 1000. You may also gain an insight into the child's understanding and use of place value by, for example, giving the child a set that includes 12 and 21 or 112 and 121.

Making numbers

page 73

Read, write and order two- and three-digit numbers At the outset, you may need to explain what a digit is.

The child should continue recording numbers until he/she thinks that all the combinations have been made. You may wish to ask the child to order only the two-digit numbers.

In order to restrict the number of possible outcomes, it will probably be necessary to stipulate that each digit can only be used once in each number. With the numbers 1, 2 and 3 it is thus possible to make 12, 21, 13, 31, 23, 32, 123, 132, 231, 213, 312 and 321.

In assessing this task (see checklist on sheet), look for the ability to read all the numbers correctly (for example, reading 21 as 'twenty-one', not 'two one' or 'twoty-one'). Also look for evidence, both in the reading and in the ordering of numbers, that the child has a good understanding of place value (for example, reading 21 as 'twenty-one' not 'twelve'). Look for evidence of a systematic approach to the problem, and awareness (in the child's comments) that only certain numbers can be made.

Nearest number

page 74

Rounding up/down to the nearest multiple of 10 This is an exciting activity which will require some understanding of place value and decade order. You will also need to have established the convention that 5 units are always rounded up rather than down.

Asking the child to claim each square by writing in the number that has been rounded up or down should provide a check that the conventions are being correctly interpreted. Though the activity can be played as a competitive game, it could also be approached as a collaborative task. The key assessment features of the activity are detailed on the sheet.

What now?

page 75

Using calculators and mental strategies The sheet needs to be tailored to the needs of the individual or group. You may opt to focus on one operation, or to leave the choice of operations open. The example below shows a sheet before and after completion. This example represents high attainment; a younger or less able child could work on a sheet which deals exclusively with number bonds within 10.

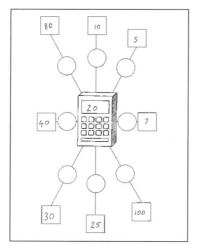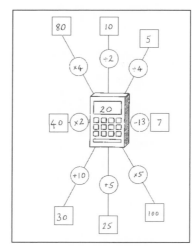

The assessment focus for this activity is observational evidence:
• the accuracy of the child's mental calculations;
• the ability to use appropriate key sequences when working with a calculator;
• the use of multiplication and/or division where appropriate.

Money

Shopping

page 76

Using money to the value of 10p If appropriate, demonstrate the correct arrangement of coins for the first item. If the child cannot appreciate that a coin might have a value other than 1, this task is too difficult for her/him. In such cases, further work needs to be done on the purchase of items with 1p coins only, followed by the introduction of the 2p coin. To engage in this task, the child needs to be able to handle money with confidence. Correct combinations might typically be found by starting with the largest appropriate denomination and building up to the required total. The able child might move on to look at coin combinations within 20p, using an adapted activity sheet.

Target price

page 77

Addition involving coins You will need to prepare a dice or spinner for each pair with coin values depending on the target amount (see Figure 2). For the target totals 50p and £1, you may decide to use fewer different types of coin than are suggested here.

Note that the child can use the same coin more than once, and need not fill all the spaces on the arrow. The players should record the race by replacing the coins on the arrow with numbers, drawings or stuck-down coin stamps. The game can be played and recorded several times, leading to discussion of different ways of making the same target total.

Target	Spinner values	
5p	1p, 2p	*Figure 2*
10p	1p, 2p, 5p	
20p	1p, 2p, 5p, 10p	
50p	1p, 2p, 5p, 10p, 20p	
£1	1p, 2p, 5p, 10p, 20p, 50p	

For observing and assessing, the following questions are important:
• Can the child identify appropriate coins and add them up to make the correct total?
• Can the child reject coins which would take her/his total beyond the coin he/she is aiming for?
• Can the child talk to you about the combinations he/she has made? Some children might also be able to tell you which way of making the amount uses the fewest coins.

Spend £1

page 78

Buying things to £1 You may wish to collect and label objects with appropriate prices for the child to use. During the task, you will have the opportunity to observe the child working out and recording totals, using equipment from a given range and using her/his own methods of calculating totals and change.

After the child has finished, talk to her/him about the methods he/she has used. Possible strategies include: using knowledge of the 2, 5 and 10 times tables; use of counting on or back; estimating and then checking. The child might work out the change by counting on from the total rather than subtracting from £1.

Born to shop

page 79

Using coin values beyond £1; using decimal notation You may prefer to use real items labelled with the appropriate prices for the children to 'buy' from a shop or post office. At this level it is important for the child to have access to real coins for this task, both as practical support for the calculations and to reinforce specific knowledge of coin values.

During the task, you should have opportunities to assess the child's use of mental methods, choice and use of appropriate equipment (coins or base 10 apparatus), recording and checking of totals. An important aspect of the task to assess is the child's use of decimal notation in her/his recording when working with amounts larger than £1. Checking with a calculator may support the child in doing this. Children who need more work on decimal notation will record without reference to it, still working in pence (for example, recording '110 pence' rather than '£1.10').

Fruit corner

page 80

Solving a money problem in a realistic context The sheet gives scope for a range of questions such as the following (which are given in order of increasing difficulty):
*   How much are an apple and a banana together?
*   How much more does an apple cost than a banana?
*   How many lemons could you buy for £1?
*   If you bought bunches of grapes, how many bunches could you buy for £1? What would your change be?
*   Can you spend exactly £1, buying at least one of everything?
*   What costs more, five apples or four lemons?
*   I bought five fruits and they were apples and bananas. The total cost was 65p. How many of each did I buy?

As an extension, you could ask the child to devise further problems and write them on the sheet for another child to solve.

Algebra

In its place

page 81

Ordinal numbers, 1st to 6th You may prefer to use toy animals for this assessment and then record the child's responses on the sheet. This task will give you the opportunity to assess whether the child can describe positions using mathematical terms (1st, 2nd, and so on), and can also respond appropriately to the words 'first', 'second', and so on.

All in order

page 82

Ordinal position and repeating patterns It is important to provide a wide range of small items with mathematical qualities including shape and size. The child should previously have had experience with practical materials (for example, beads or buttons). When the child has filled the track with a repeating pattern, ask her/him whether there is anything special about the ordinal positions of (for example) the squares or the red counters. In an alternating pattern, the link will be related to odd and even numbers. Patterns with a repeat of 3 or more will be linked to the corresponding multiplication facts. Ask the child to explain her/his predictions for the 10th, 15th and 20th positions, to identify whether awareness of pattern can be carried forward (for example, 'It will be blue because 15 is in the 3 times table').

A younger or less able child might typically describe the pattern as he/she sees it (for example, 'It goes blue, red, blue, red...'). An older child may begin to use mathematical language to describe the pattern (for example, 'It repeats after every three times'). Such a child may have some success in making predictions: a correct response will suggest that he/she is able to generalise.

Round and round

page 83

Recognising and creating repeating patterns This activity develops ideas similar to those introduced on page 82, and the child will use the same or similar materials (such as buttons or small shapes) to generate a repeating pattern. The use of a closed or circular pattern of 12 elements allows patterns with a repeat every 2, 3, 4 or 6 elements. It is important to draw the child's attention to the endlessly repeating nature of the closed pattern.

The assessment will depend on the child's ability to make a repeating pattern and describe it in mathematical terms. Ask the child questions to assess this understanding – for example:
• 'Tell me about your pattern. How often does it repeat itself?'
• 'Could you label the oval numbers like a clock? What is the link between these numbers and (say) the red shapes?'
• 'Why does it work with patterns of 3?'
• 'What other repeating patterns will work? Patterns of 4? Why?'

Pick a pair

page 84

Adding pairs of consecutive numbers and identifying a general rule Make sure that the child has understood that the activity is confined to adding numbers which are 'next to each other' on the number line. The space on the sheet will allow the child to record all the combinations as number sentences (for example, 3 + 4 = 7).

This assessment allows you to check the child's ability to add two numbers accurately and to spot a general pattern. The former task will occupy children who are at an early stage of computation, while the latter should be something which the able child achieves (making a statement such as 'The total will always be odd'). You might assess the child further by asking a question which goes beyond the range on the sheet (for example, 'If you add 99 to 100, will it be odd or even? Why?') Some children may still be at the stage of needing materials for counting. The checklist on the sheet offers several pointers for assessment, including the option of working outside the range 0–9.

Up and down

page 85

Counting in steps of 2, 5 and 10 Decide the range of numbers to be assessed. The sheet can be piecemeal: it is possible to return to the sheet at different points, or to use the whole sheet for revision when appropriate (perhaps later in the key stage).

The first two tasks can be recorded on the number lines provided. The other tasks may be carried out on a longer number line, and the numbers landed on recorded in the spaces on the sheet. Note any comments the child makes on the patterns that occur (for example, patterns of odd and even numbers; the 0, 5, 0, 5 units pattern when counting in 5s).

Number chains

page 86

Using different operations to complete a number chain This task is differentiated by:
• the size of the start/finish number;
• the operations to be used in the intermediate stages.

A child lacking broad experience of number operations will work with small numbers and use only addition and subtraction to complete the sequence. A child who has been introduced to multiplication may add this element to the work, and will thus need to use division to complete the chain. The most able child may need to be encouraged to be adventurous in the scale of the numbers in the intermediate stages, and the range of operations deployed. Such a child could be restricted to using only multiplication and division.

Name *Date*

Numbers

Using and applying
• *Uses materials provided for task.*
• *Talks about own work.*

Ask the child to tell you about numbers he/she knows about, such as his/ her age, house number, birthday and phone number. Scribe the answers. Ask the child to record some of her/his counting by drawing familiar objects. Count orally forwards and backwards, encouraging the child to go as far as she/he can.

Note how far the child can count orally:
❑ 0 → 10
❑ 0 → 20
❑ 10 → 0
❑ 20 → 0
The child counts objects accurately to ❑

Teacher comments:

Some numbers I know about:

I counted some

_____

There were

_____

I counted some

_____

There were

_____

I can count from _____ to _____

I can count back from _____ to _____

Demonstrates that the child can count to 50 or to 100, write numbers to 50 or to 100 and count forwards or backwards.

Using and applying
• Selects and uses appropriate maths for a task (counting).
• Checks work.
• Organises a task.

Provide four collections of the same objects for the child to count. Ask the child to record her/his totals, and draw one of whatever they counted, in the speech bubbles.

Note whether the child:
❑ can count to 50
❑ can count to 100

Teacher comments:

Teachers' notes, page 22

Count it!

I counted

I can count to ____

I can count back from ____

Name   *Date*

Spotty snakes

Demonstrates that the child can count and record the count in written numerals.

Using and applying
• Selects and uses appropriate maths for a task (counting).

Before copying this sheet, draw spots on the snakes. Ask the child to count the spots and record in the boxes.

Note whether the child:
❑ can count accurately
❑ can record correctly
Range: _____ to
_____

Teacher comments:

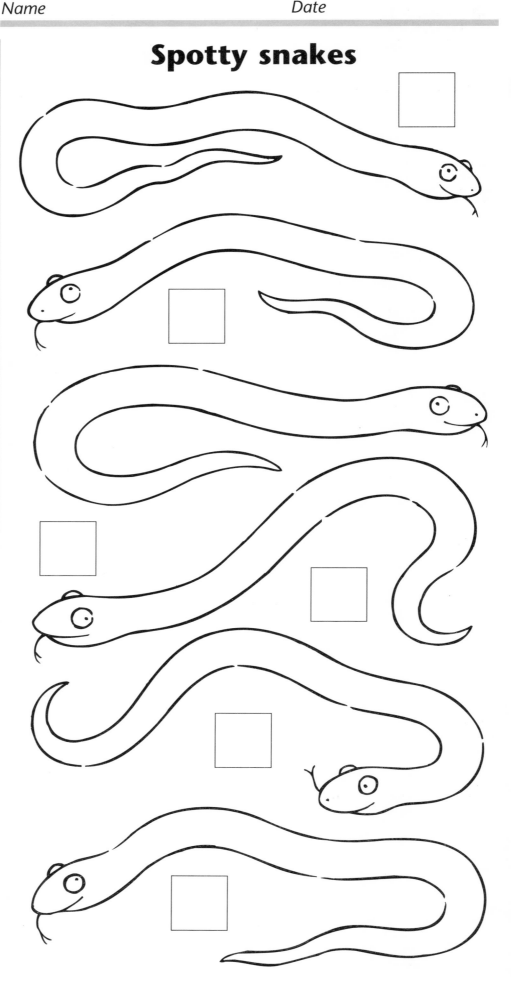

Teachers' notes, pages 22–23

SCHOLASTIC PORTFOLIO ASSESSMENT
Maths Key Stage 1

Name _____   *Date* _____

Guess how many!

Demonstrates that the child can estimate sensibly within a given range and count accurately to check.

Using and applying
• *Uses own experience.*
• *Checks own work.*

Tell the children the range within which the amounts fall: 'No more than...' and 'No less than...'. Then ask the child to make an estimate of each amount, write it down and check it by counting.

Note whether the child's estimates:
❑ are sensible
❑ are wild
❑ become more plausible during the task
❑ are checked by accurate counting

Teacher comments:

My guess: about [ ]

When I counted: [ ]

My guess: about [ ]

When I counted: [ ]

My guess: about [ ]

When I counted: [ ]

My guess: about [ ]

When I counted: [ ]

My guess: about [ ]

When I counted: [ ]

My guess: about [ ]

When I counted: [ ]

Teachers' notes, page 23

Demonstrates that the child can count larger numbers in groups or steps.

Using and applying
• *Devises a method to carry out the investigation.*
• *Modifies the method with experience.*
• *Estimates sensibly.*
• *Works co-operatively with a partner.*
• *Explains methods.*

Give each pair of children a pot of seeds. Ask the pair to discuss and estimate the number of seeds, and then to describe how they are going to find out the number. Scribe for each child where necessary. Note the strategies the child uses, and any changes the child wishes to make to his/her estimate as he/she counts.

Teacher comments:

Teachers' notes, pages 23–24

Name _____ *Date* _____

Counting up

I worked with _____

How many seeds in your pot? Our guess: ☐

How we are going to find out:

What we did:

What we found out:

The maths we used:

Name

Date

Do they match?

Demonstrates that the child can match one-to-one and recognise where there is 'one more'.

Using and applying
• Responds to questions.

Use the initial mapping of cup to saucer on the sheet to show the child how to start the matching. For each section, ask the child how many more of which object he/she needs to make a matching set. Encourage the child to draw or write the required items in the spaces provided. Discuss the numbers of the items.

Note whether the child:
❑ matches one to one
❑ works without support
❑ identifies which set has more items for each section

Teacher comments:

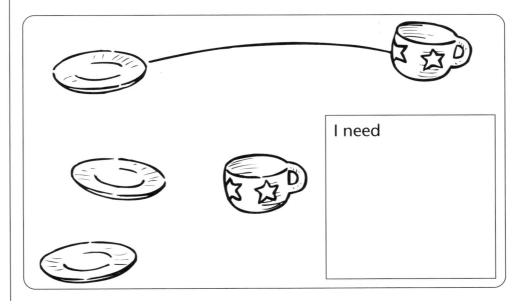

Teachers' notes, page 24

Name   *Date*

Hit-a-six

Demonstrates the child's
ability to match numerals
(1–6) to their numerical
values.

Using and applying
• *Follows a set of rules.*
• *Works with others and
discusses the game.*
• *Develops strategies.*

Two game boards are
provided to let each child
record two attempts at
the game. Each group
will also need a dice with
the numerals 1–6 and
some coloured pencils.

Rules (2–4 players)
•   Take turns to roll the
dice. Colour (or cover
with cubes) the
appropriate number of
squares in any one strip.
•   For each turn, the
player may only enter
that score on the board if
a large enough space is
available on one of the
strips.
•   The winner is the first
to fill the whole game
board.

Note whether the child:
❑ matches dice numbers
to spaces on the sheet
❑ can count the scores
needed to finish
❑ begins to develop
game strategies

Teacher comments:

Game 1

Game 2

Teachers' notes, page 24

Demonstrates the child's ability to count on from one number to another.

Using and applying
• *Works systematically.*
• *Records in a tabular format.*

Prepare the 'finish' column by entering the same target number (9 or more) in each space. Label the number line (with counting numbers in ascending order), ensuring that it ends with the target number. For example, if the 'finish' target is 9, label the line 0–9; if the 'finish' target is 15, label the line 6–15.

Demonstrate how to fill in a line of the table. Then ask the child to start from different points along the line, entering each start number in the 'start' column, and count on to the given target number. For each start number, the child should record the number of jumps required in the middle column.

Note whether the child:
❑ can count on from one number to another
❑ works independently
❑ recognises the link to addition across each row

Teacher comments:

Teachers' notes, page 24

Hop it!

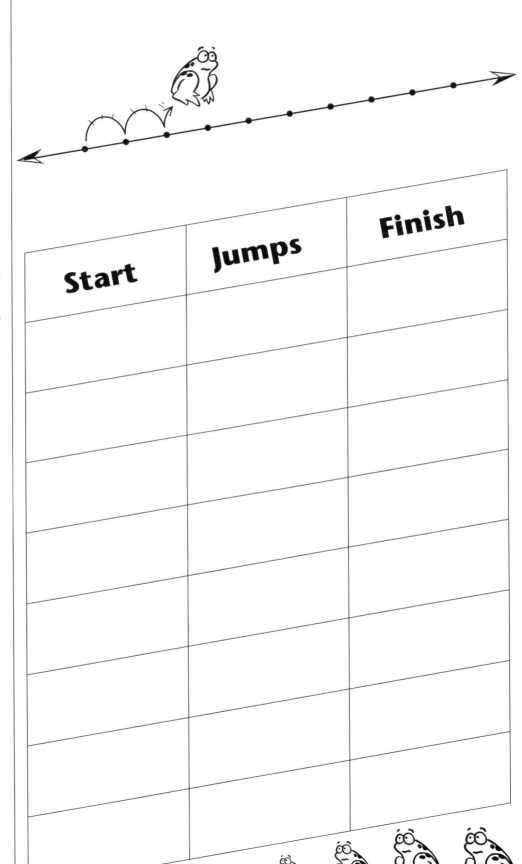

Start	Jumps	Finish

Name _____ *Date* _____

Follow my rule

The rule is: _____

_____

Demonstrates the child's ability to match one number to another according to given criteria.

Using and applying
• *Uses the materials provided.*
• *Selects the mathematics.*
• *Talks about the work done.*

Prepare this sheet (before photocopying) by writing in the rule and two sets of numbers such that the numbers can be paired up by a common connecting rule. Demonstrate how the connection provided follows the rule (for example, 4 connected to 6 where the rule is 'The total is 10'). Ask the child to make the remaining connections. Provide suitable counting materials such as Multilink cubes or number lines.

Note whether the child:
❏ follow the given rule
❏ calculates accurately with materials
❏ calculates accurately without materials

Teacher comments:

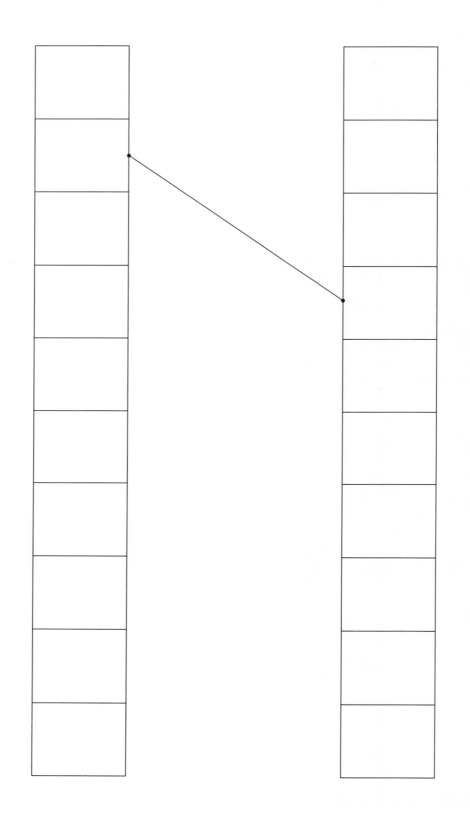

Teachers' notes, page 25

Name _____ *Date* _____

Spot the difference

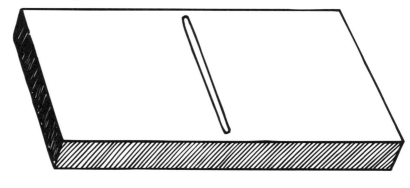

Using and applying
• *Works systematically.*
• *Records work in symbolic or pictorial form.*

Choose a number of counters (for example, 6) to represent domino spots. Place them on the large domino at the top of the sheet. Ask the child to find different combinations of the spots across the two halves of the domino (for example, 2 and 4) and to record these. Ask the child whether all the possible combinations have been found, and scribe her/his response if necessary.

Note whether the child:
❑ finds some combinations
❑ finds all the combinations
❑ records independently
❑ works systematically

Teacher comments:

Have you found all the combinations? _____

How do you know? _____

_____

_____

Teachers' notes, page 25

Name   *Date*

Make it up I

Demonstrates the child's ability to represent a number in several different ways.

Using and applying
- ***Selects the mathematics for the task.***
- ***Represents a number with pictures and/or symbols.***
- ***Identifies a pattern for generating number facts.***

Prepare and photocopy this sheet with a number on the spider (for example, 3). Provide suitable materials such as Multilink cubes or number lines. Ask the child to identify different ways of showing that number, for example:
pictorial ∝ ∝ ∝
numerical 5 − 2
They should record their answers at the ends of the 'legs'.

Note whether the child:
❑ uses pictures
❑ uses computation
❑ uses materials
❑ calculates mentally
❑ identifies a generating sequence

Teacher comments:

Teachers' notes, page 25

Name

Date

Now you see it...

Demonstrates the child's
ability to use
complementary addition.

Using and applying
• *Talks about the work
using mathematical
vocabulary.*
• *Makes predictions.*

Arrange a given number
of cubes (or counters)
evenly, but randomly
within the large outline.
Sit opposite the child so
that the sheet is upside-
down for you. Partition
the set into two groups,
using a sheet of card to
hide one of these groups
from the child. Ask the
child to tell you how
many cubes he/she can
see, and then to write in
the first box how many
he/she thinks you can
see. Repeat and record
four more times.

Note whether the child:
❏ counts cubes
accurately
❏ predicts with accuracy
❏ discusses the work
❏ uses knowledge of
number bonds

Teacher comments:

My guess

☐ ☐ ☐ ☐ ☐

My check

☐ ☐ ☐ ☐ ☐

Teachers' notes, page 26

Name   Date

Mix and match I

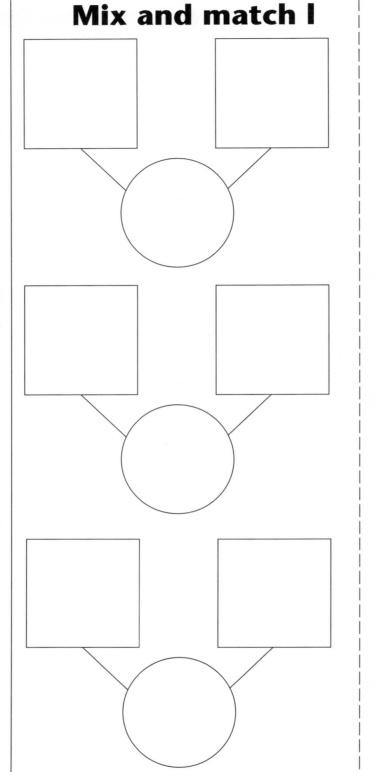

Demonstrates the child's ability to recall and use addition bonds.

Using and applying
• *Uses appropriate materials.*
• *Selects mathematics for the task.*
• *Identifies cases where more than one solution is possible.*
• *Finds solutions using a strategy.*

Prepare the sheet by adding numbers (see Teachers' notes) to the nine shapes around the edge of the page. Provide suitable counting materials such as Multilink cubes or number lines. Tell the child to cut out and arrange the numbers so that, for each of the three sets, the sum of the two squares is represented in the circle. Stick down her/his solution on the sheet as a permanent record.

Note whether the child:
❑ adds accurately
❑ uses apparatus (cubes)
❑ uses mental methods
❑ uses trial and improvement (or another strategy)

Teacher comments:

Teachers' notes, page 26

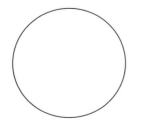
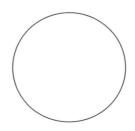
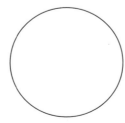

Name

Date

Does it add up?

51

Demonstrates the child's ability to add three numbers together in the context of a problem-solving task.

Using and applying
• *Selects the mathematics for the task.*
• *Finds ways of overcoming difficulties.*
• *Discusses/communicates solutions.*

Prepare this sheet before copying by writing the numbers (see Teachers' notes) in the five squares at the bottom of the sheet. The task is to cut out these squares and arrange them on the grid so that the horizontal total is the same as the vertical total. The child should record successful arrangements in the four small grids. When the task is completed, the child should paste her/his 'favourite' solution on the larger grid.

Note whether the child:
❑ uses trial and improvement
❑ uses and explains this strategy
❑ calculates accurately

Teacher comments:

My answers:

Teachers' notes, pages 26–27

✂ —

Demonstrates the child's ability to solve problems involving an addition grid.

Using and applying
• *Selects the mathematics for the task.*
• *Works systematically.*

Before copying the sheet, label all of the rectangles with the chosen number pair (see Teachers' notes). Ask the child to write numbers in the circles to complete the addition grids, using different numbers each time. For example:

④ ⑥
③ 7 9

Note whether the child:
❑ finds several solutions
❑ uses addition
❑ uses subtraction
❑ works independently

Teacher comments:

Teachers' notes, page 27

Double hit

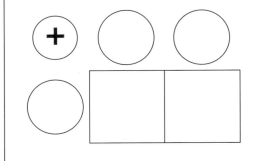

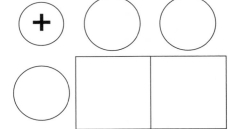

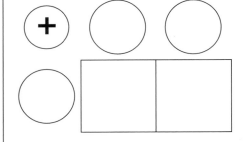

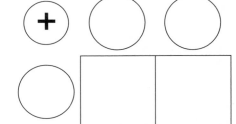

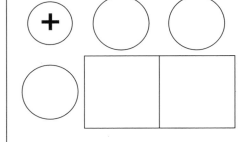

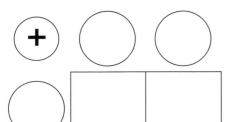

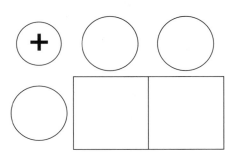

Name

Date

Does it add up again?

Demonstrates the child's ability to add several numbers together. Demonstrates that the child can solve problems using addition.

Using and applying
• *Selects the mathematics for the task.*
• *Finds ways to overcome difficulties.*
• *Finds several solutions to the problem.*

Cut out the numeral tiles below. Ask the child to arrange the nine numerals on the cross (right) so that both diagonals have the same total. He/she should find several arrangements, recording them on the smaller crosses; finally, he/she can record a 'favourite' solution by sticking the numerals down on the large cross.

Note whether the child:
❑ adds accurately
❑ uses knowledge of number patterns
❑ finds at least one solution
❑ explains her/his work

Teacher comments:

Teachers' notes, page 27

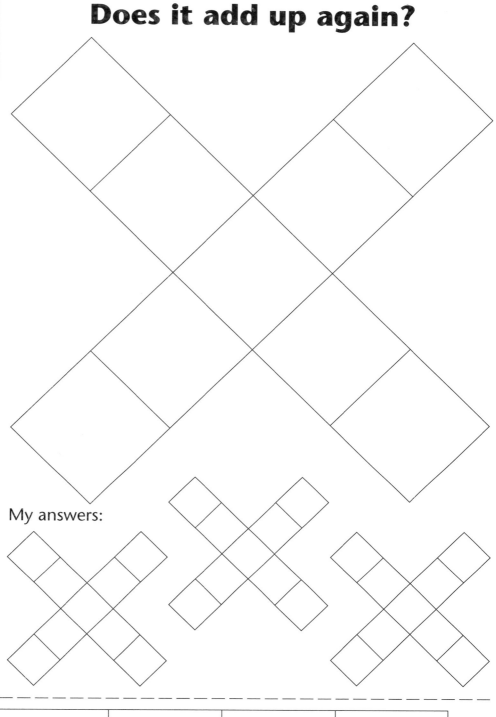

My answers:

1	2	3	4	5
6	7	8	9	

Name

Date

Pictures and words

*Demonstrates the child's
ability to contextualise an
arithmetic sum in words
or pictures.*

Using and applying
* *Selects the
mathematics for a task.*
* *Talks about the work.*

Prepare the sheet by
writing appropriate
numerical problems (for
example, 6 + 2, 10 ÷ 2) in
the top left-hand box of
each of the three panels.
Ask the child to draw a
picture to represent the
problem, or to write a
number 'story' in words.
(See Teachers' notes.) He/
she should complete the
sheet by writing the
answers in the boxes at
the bottom right of each
panel.

Note whether the child:
❏ completes the sheet
with no support
❏ completes the sheet
with support
❏ uses mental methods
of calculation only
❏ uses apparatus for
calculation

Teacher comments:

Teachers' notes, pages
27–28

SCHOLASTIC PORTFOLIO ASSESSMENT
Maths Key Stage 1

Name

Date

Up and away

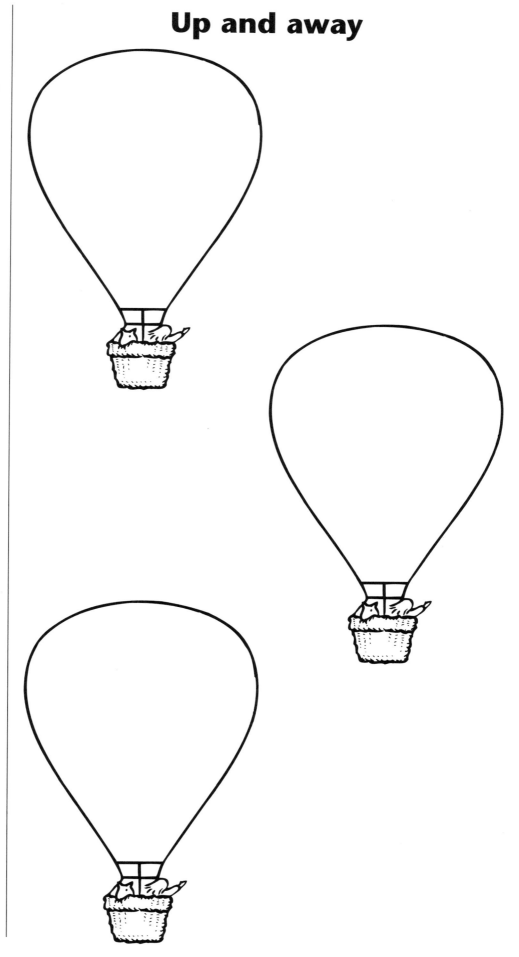

Demonstrates the child's ability to partition a given total between three subsets, and to record the different arrangements.

Using and applying
• **Works flexibly with numbers.**
• **Communicates results.**
• **Uses knowledge of number patterns to generate different combinations.**

Ask the child to arrange a given set of cubes or counters in different ways by distributing them between the three balloons. He/she should record the combinations in the spaces around the balloons. Finally, the balloons can be coloured in to represent one of the solutions.

Note whether the child:
❑ records appropriately
❑ uses a systematic method to generate new arrangements
❑ discusses the work

Teacher comments:

Teachers' notes, page 28

Demonstrates the child's ability to add two 2-digit numbers, and arrange the numbers to find the largest/smallest total.

Using and applying
• **Selects equipment to support the work.**
• **Finds several solutions to the task.**

Prepare four number cards by writing digits in the four squares on the right of this sheet. Give one copy of the sheet to each child. Provide some appropriate number equipment such as Multibase or Multilink. Ask the child to arrange the four number cards on the addition grid and then calculate the answer, showing the sum and the total in the space provided. The child should try to find all the possible combinations and answers, then record the largest and smallest totals he/she can find at the bottom of the sheet.

Note whether the child:
❑ uses apparatus
❑ works confidently
❑ identifies the largest total
❑ identifies the smallest total
❑ finds all possible combinations

Teacher comments:

Teachers' notes, page 28

Name

Date

How many ways?

$+$

The largest total is _____

The smallest total is _____

Name   *Date*

Add or take away?

4 ◯ 3 = 7

5 ◯ 2 = 3

4 ◯ 4 = 8

5 ◯ 3 = 2

5 ◯ 1 = 6

8 ◯ 6 = 2

9 ◯ 3 = 6

2 ◯ 8 = 10

1 ◯ 6 = 7

7 ◯ 6 = 1

Demonstrates that the child can choose the correct operation to complete a number sentence. Demonstrates that the child can use number bonds to 10.

Using and applying
• *Chooses appropriate equipment.*
• *Explains her/his own methods.*
• *Recognises patterns.*
• *Makes appropriate generalisations.*

Ask the child to decide whether the correct operation to complete the number sentence in each case is + or –. Allow the child to use cubes or a number line if he/she wishes to.

Note whether the child:
❑ completes the number sentences accurately
❑ uses apparatus
❑ works mentally

Teacher comments:

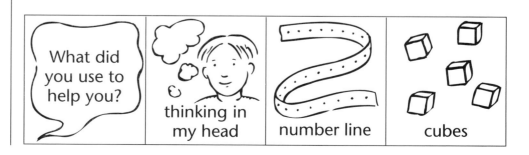

What did you use to help you?   thinking in my head   number line   cubes

Demonstrates the child's ability to work with different number operations.

Using and applying
• *Works flexibly with numbers.*
• *Selects the mathematics for a task.*
• *Records work in a symbolic form.*

Prepare the sheet (before copying) by writing numerals in the five rectangles. Provide suitable number materials, such as Multibase or Multilink cubes. Demonstrate what to do using the two linked rectangles (see Teachers' notes). Tell the child to make further links and to use each pair of numbers to create a x, + and/or – calculation.

Note whether the child:
❑ uses addition
❑ uses subtraction
❑ uses multiplication
❑ identifies the largest and smallest possible answers
❑ records his/her work
❑ works independently
❑ requires materials

Teacher comments:

Name _____   Date _____

Making links

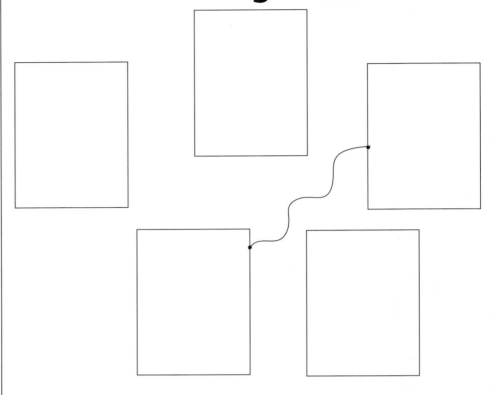

I used these operations:

I made these calculations:

Which calculation gives the largest answer? _____

Which calculation gives the smallest answer? _____

Teachers' notes, page 29

Name

Date

Demonstrates the child's ability to see subtraction in terms of 'taking away'.

Using and applying
• *Use mathematics in the context of a story problem.*
• *Records symbolically.*

Cut out the bears from the edge of the sheet. Place some or all of them on the mat, and place the corresponding number card in the first box of the number sentence. Ask the child to make up 'subtraction stories' in which some bears leave the picnic and others stay. He/she should then use small number cards to represent the story in the spaces provided, and record the number facts in the box below (for example, 10 – 6 = 4). Finally, the child should paste down some cut-out bears on the mat and write a suitable number story below it.

Note whether the child:
❑ works independently
❑ identifies the link between addition and subtraction
❑ generates several number sentences from a given starting number
❑ can predict answers to subtractions.

Teacher comments:

Teachers' notes, page 29

The bear facts

$$\square - \square = \square$$

My number stories

Demonstrates the child's ability to calculate differences between numbers and to recognise patterns.

Using and applying
• *Finds several combinations.*
• *Presents combinations in pictorial or symbolic form.*
• *Notices a pattern in the answers.*

Provide each child with a copy of this sheet and a length of 10 interlocking cubes. Demonstrate the example and encourage the child to find different examples, each time recording the lengths and the difference between them. Can he/she identify a pattern in the answers?

Note whether the child:
❑ finds differences accurately
❑ recognises a pattern in the answers
❑ records independently

Teacher comments:

Name _____   Date _____

Make it, break it

A 10 stick can be broken like this:

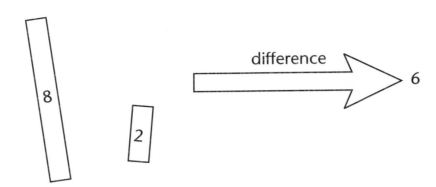

Try breaking the 10 stick in different ways.
What is the difference between the two pieces?

What did you notice? _____

_____

_____

Teachers' notes, pages 29–30

NUMBER, MONEY & ALGEBRA

Demonstrates the child's ability to partition (share) a number of objects into two or three subsets, and to identify a pattern.

Using and applying
• *Talks about the work using mathematical language.*
• *Predicts accurately which numbers will partition with no remainder.*

Prepare this sheet (before copying) by partitioning the circle into two halves or three thirds. Try the first number (6) by seeing whether six cubes (or counters) can be shared equally between the subsets. Write a X below the number. Let the child continue with the other numbers. Use the second grid to write some different numbers to challenge the child appropriately.

Note whether the child:
❑ works without support
❑ shares the cubes correctly
❑ can predict and/or generalise results

Teacher comments:

Fair shares?

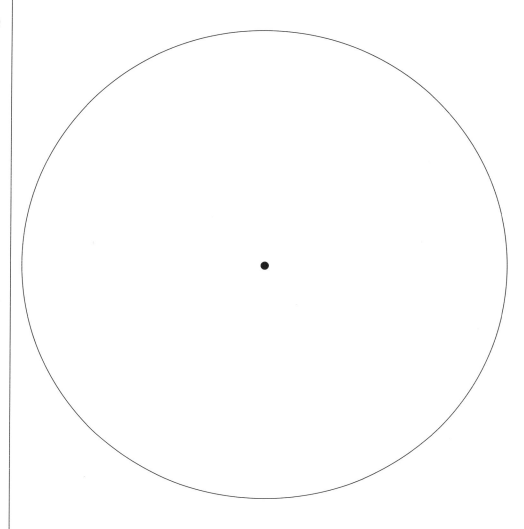

6	4	7	8	5

Teachers' notes, page 30

Demonstrates the child's ability to identify halves and quarters of a whole.

Using and applying
• Uses correct mathematical terminology.
• Finds different combinations to create a whole.

Cut out the pieces of shaded circles from the right-hand edge of the sheet. Ask the child to find three *different* ways of filling a blank circle on the sheet by pasting some of the shaded pieces into it. Talk to the child about the fractions he/she has used. See Teachers' notes for the game option.

Note whether the child:
❑ uses the words 'half' and 'quarter'
❑ finds three different ways of making a whole

Teacher comments:

Teachers' notes, page 30

62

Name

Date

Make it up II

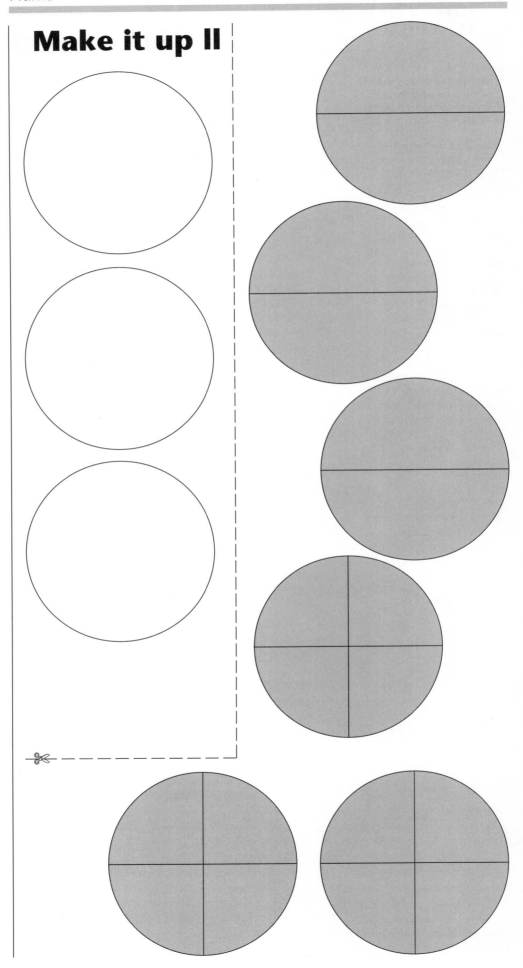

Sharing out

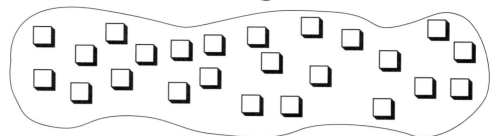

NUMBER, MONEY & ALGEBRA

Demonstrates that the child can share a group of objects into equal sets and record formally using a ÷ sign.

Using and applying
- *Organises and checks work.*
- *Recognises patterns and relationships.*

Give the child 24 cubes. Ask her/him to find some ways of making equal groupings by sharing them out. Ask the child to record her/his work both pictorially and in the form of calculations (if he/she can).

Note whether the child:
❑ makes equal groups
❑ records each arrangement in his/her own way
❑ records formally using a ÷ sign

Teacher comments:

Teachers' notes, pages 30–31

NUMBER, MONEY & ALGEBRA

Demonstrates the child's ability to solve problems involving multiplication and division.

Using and applying
* *Uses mental strategies.*
* *Uses trial and improvement.*

Prepare the lower section of the sheet by writing the same single-digit number in each of the boxes in the top row (eg 4). Write a different number in the second row (eg 3). The number in the bottom row must be the product of these two numbers (in this case, 12).

Photocopy the sheet. Ask the child to cut and arrange these numbers in the upper section to make four different number sentences, two multiplication and two division. All four number sentences must be true. When they have checked their solutions, they can stick them in place.

Note whether the child:
❑ calculates mentally
❑ uses apparatus
❑ uses trial and improvement

Teacher comments:

Mix and match II

$$\Box \times \Box = \Box$$

$$\Box \times \Box = \Box$$

$$\Box \div \Box = \Box$$

$$\Box \div \Box = \Box$$

Teachers' notes, page 31

Name

Date

Bits and pieces

My dice throws

My score

Demonstrates the child's ability to find $\frac{1}{2}$ and $\frac{1}{4}$ of a quantity.

Using and applying
• **Selects mathematics for the task.**
• **Uses the correct mathematical terms.**

This activity is a game for 2–4 players. Provide two dice labelled $\frac{1}{2}$, $\frac{1}{2}$, $\frac{1}{2}$, $\frac{1}{4}$, $\frac{1}{4}$, $\frac{1}{4}$ and 0, 4, 4, 8, 8, 12. Each player or pair (see Teachers' notes) has an individual copy of the sheet. The players take turns to roll both dice and colour in the number of circles equal to the quantity indicated by both dice. For example, $\frac{1}{2}$ of 8 = 4. After eight rounds, add up the number of circles coloured in to establish who has won.

Note whether the child:
❑ can calculate $\frac{1}{2}$ of a quantity
❑ can calculate $\frac{1}{4}$ of a quantity
❑ describes the methods he/she has used

Teacher comments:

My total score was _____

I came 🏅1ST 🏅2ND 🏅3RD 🏅4TH _____

Demonstrates that the child can work mentally with numbers.

Using and applying
• *Selects and uses the appropriate maths.*

Ask the child to answer your questions on the sheet, one by one. Remind the child that he/she can write or draw the answer, and may use apparatus. Then read out the ten questions.

Note whether the child performs the following successfully:
❏ 1, 2, 3 – counting accurately
❏ 4, 5 – finding numbers before and after
❏ 6, 7 – ordering
❏ 8 – adding
❏ 9 – subtracting
❏ 10 – identifying a pattern

Teacher comments:

Name

Date

Thinking about maths I

1.

2.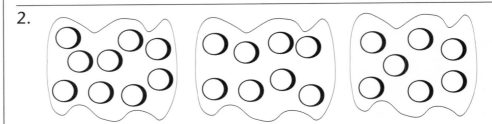

3.

4.   5.

6.   7.

8.   9.

10.

Teachers' notes, page 31

Name   *Date*

Thinking about maths II

Demonstrates that the child can work mentally with numbers.

Using and applying
• *Selects and uses the appropriate maths.*

Ask the child to answer your questions on the sheet, one by one. Remind them that he/she or she can write or draw the answer, and may use apparatus. Then read out the ten questions.

Note whether the child performs the following successfully:
❑ 1 – counting accurately
❑ 2, 3 – recalling number bonds
❑ 4, 5 – ordering with awareness of place value
❑ 6 – finding $\frac{1}{2}$ of a number
❑ 7 – distinguishing between odd and even numbers
❑ 8 – choosing an operation (+)
❑ 9 – choosing an operation (–)
❑ 10 – counting in tens and units

Teacher comments:

1.

2.

3.

4.

5.

6.

7.

8.

9.

10.
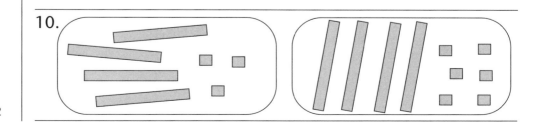

Teachers' notes, page 32

NUMBER, MONEY & ALGEBRA

Demonstrates that the child can order numbers between 0 and 10.

Using and applying
• Understands and uses mathematical language; more than/less than; before/after; next.

Ask the child to listen to the number you say and tell you the number before it. Work through six numbers, using both 'before' and 'after' questions. Then ask the child to draw numbers as he/she visualises them when answering the questions. Finally, ask the child to draw her/his mental image of the number line. You may need to scribe for the child.

Can the child:
❑ order numbers between 0 and 10

respond to the terms:
❑ more than
❑ less than
❑ before
❑ after
❑ next

Teacher comments:

Before and after

My number line

Teachers' notes, page 32

Name   *Date*

In my head

Demonstrates that the child can add and subtract mentally. Demonstrates the child's instant recall of number bonds.

Using and applying
• *Explains her/his own methods.*

For each box on the sheet, give the child a starting number (verbally) and then ask her/him to add another number on to or take it away from the first number mentally. Scribe the child's answers on the sheet (if appropriate). Finally, ask the child to explain and draw (in either pictorial or numerical form) how he/ she visualised one of the calculations.

Note whether the child:
❏ adds accurately
❏ subtracts accurately
❏ responds instantly
❏ responds with thought

Teacher comments:

Teachers' notes, pages 32–33

Demonstrates that the child can recall number facts from _____ to _____ and apply the operation required.

For each box, ask the child to start at a particular number, perform a series of operations and arrive at the end number. Record the child's answer in a cloud at each step in the string of operations. For the last set of operations, ask the child to record her/his answers in any way he/she chooses. Finally, ask her/him to draw and write what he/she did to work out one of the challenges.

Note whether the child:
❑ adds accurately
❑ subtracts accurately
❑ responds instantly
❑ responds with thought

Work it out

This is what I did:

Teachers' notes, page 33

Name   *Date*

Many times over

2×	5×	10×
_____ _____	_____ _____	_____ _____
_____ _____	_____ _____	_____ _____
_____ _____	_____ _____	_____ _____
_____ _____	_____ _____	_____ _____
_____ _____	_____ _____	_____ _____

Demonstrates the child's ability to recall and use multiplication facts. Demonstrates the child's understanding of the commutative aspect of multiplication.

Using and applying
• *Uses mental methods flexibly.*

In the first part of the task, test the child on her/his instant recall of multiplication facts. Ask the child to record only the answers on the lines provided. In the second part of the task, ask sets of questions which include using multiplication facts in mental calculations (see Teachers' notes). Finally, ask the child to explain to you how he/she worked out one of the series of calculations.

Note whether the child can recall and use:
☐ x _____ facts
☐ x _____ facts
☐ x _____ facts
☐ can work mentally

Teacher comments:

Teachers' notes, page 33

Name   *Date*

Which comes first?

Put your numbers in order. Write them in the boxes.

Demonstrates that the child can order numbers within the range _____ to _____ .

Using and applying
• *Works methodically.*
• *Uses apparatus appropriately.*

Ask the child to order a set of five number cards. He/she should work independently, recording the ordered numbers on the sheet. Give the child another three sets to order. With the last set, give the child several more number cards and ask her/him to use the circles to fit another four numbers into the square.

Note whether the child:
❑ successfully orders numbers from _____ to _____
❑ successfully places numbers in between

Teacher comments:

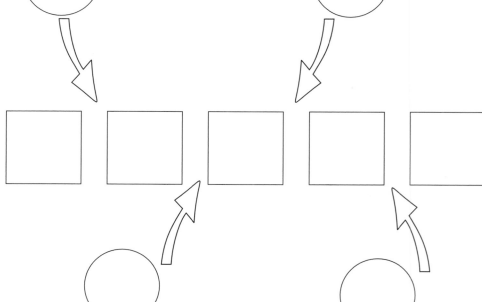

Teachers' notes, page 33

SCHOLASTIC PORTFOLIO ASSESSMENT
Maths Key Stage 1

Demonstrates that the child can make, read and write two- and three- digit numbers and order numbers up to 100/1000. Demonstrate the child's understanding of place value.

Using and applying
- *Works methodically.*
- *Uses numbers flexibly.*
- *Explains findings.*
- *Finds all possible outcomes.*

Give the child three digit cards. Ask her/him to combine those to make as many different two- and three-digit numbers as possible, recording them on the sheet. Then ask the child to read out the numbers and order them on the number lines, commenting on her/his findings.

Note whether the child:
❏ makes numbers
❏ reads them out correctly
❏ writes them correctly
❏ orders them correctly
❏ works randomly
❏ works methodically
❏ finds all possible combinations

Teacher comments:

Teachers' notes, page 34

Name   *Date*

Making numbers

My digits are:

The numbers I can make are:

I put all my numbers in order:

0 —————————————————————— 100

101 ———————————————————— 1000

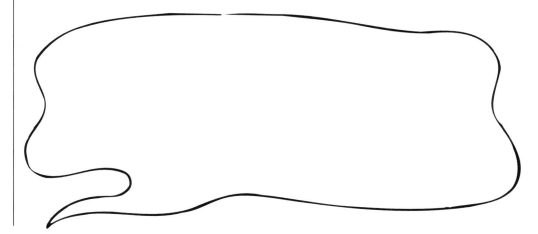

Name

Date

Nearest number

This is a game for 2–4 players. Each player needs a copy of the sheet. The group needs two dice labelled 0, 1, 2, 4, 6, 8 and 1, 3, 5, 7, 9. Players take turns to roll both dice and use the digits to generate a two-digit number (for example, 1 and 5 could be used to make 15 or 51). The player rounds her/his number up or down to the nearest multiple of 10 and claims the space occupied by that number (if vacant) by writing in the two-digit number. The first player to cover all her/his squares is the winner.

40	80
10	30
50	70
20	90
	60

I played with: _____

_____

I came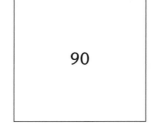

Name _____   Date _____

What now?

Demonstrates the child's ability to use calculators and mental strategies within the same task.

Using and applying
• *Selects the mathematics for the task.*
• *Checks her/his work.*

Prepare the sheet by writing a 'start' number in the calculator display box. Write a range of numbers in the square boxes around the edge of the diagram. Provide each child with a copy of the sheet and a calculator. Explain that the task is to write in each circle the operation and quantity required to change the display number into each of the target totals.

Note whether the child:
❏ selects the appropriate mathematics
❏ checks her/his work
❏ talks about her/his work

Teacher comments:

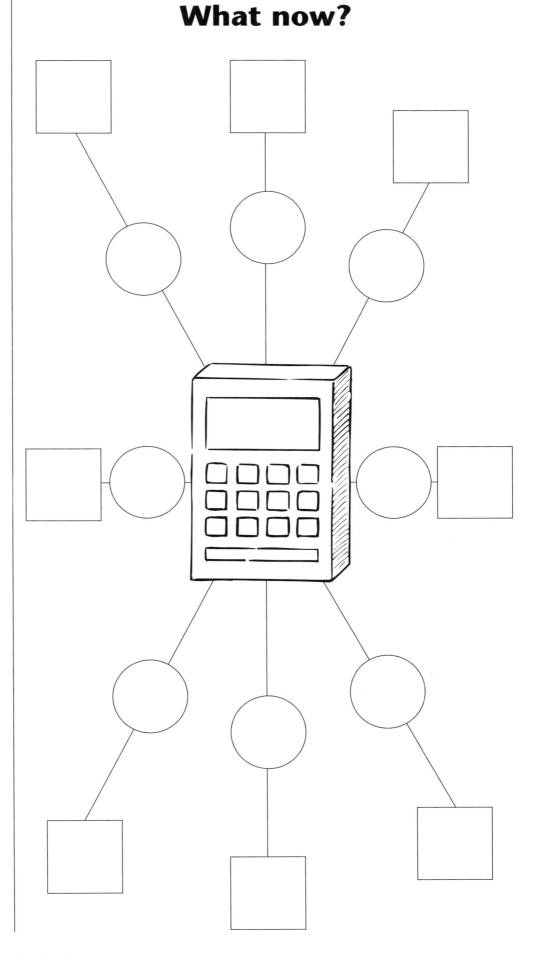

Teachers' notes, page 34

Name

Date

Shopping

Demonstrates the child's ability to use money to the value of 10p, including selecting coins to make up values.

Using and applying
• *Selects appropriate coins.*
• *Uses language in context.*
• *Records in a tabular format.*

The child needs four coins: 1p, 2p, 2p and 5p. Explain that the task is to 'buy' items using these coins. For each item, ask the child to place the coins needed and the coins remaining in the appropriate boxes. Let the child record each answer on the sheet, using coin stamps, gummed coins or drawings, before going on to the next item.

Note whether the child:
❑ understands coin denominations
❑ uses coins confidently
❑ uses appropriate mathematical language

Teacher comments:

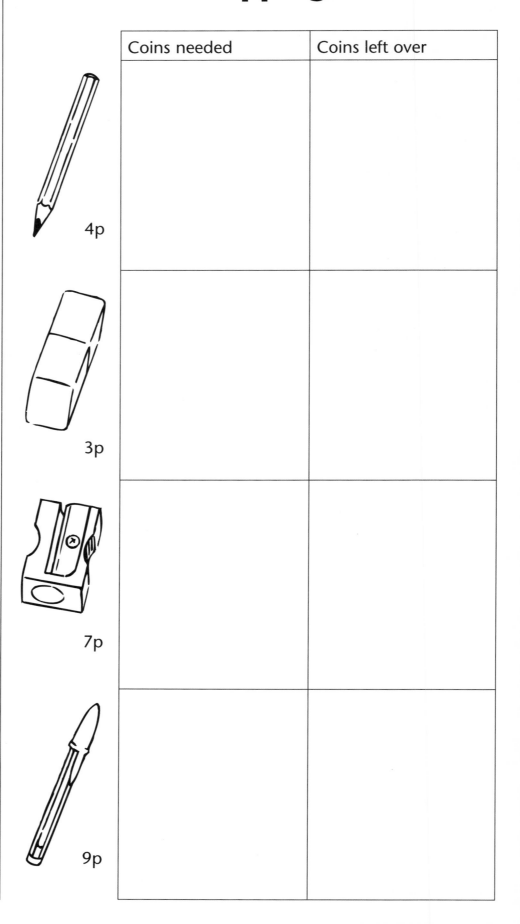

Coins needed	Coins left over

4p

3p

7p

9p

Teachers' notes, page 35

SCHOLASTIC PORTFOLIO ASSESSMENT
Maths Key Stage 1

Name   *Date*

Target price

Demonstrates that the child can add, using coins to the value of _____ and identify the right coin to end with the required value.

Using and applying
• Talks about alternative combinations.

This is a game for two players. Write the same target price on both arrows before copying the sheet; give one copy to each pair, along with a dice (or spinner) with coin values on it and some coins (or coin stamps). Players take turns to throw the dice and collect a coin, aiming to make up the target total exactly. They do not have to take a coin for each throw. Successful coin combinations can be recorded on the sheet.

Note whether the child:
❑ adds coins accurately
❑ counts on

Teacher comments:

Teachers' notes, page 35

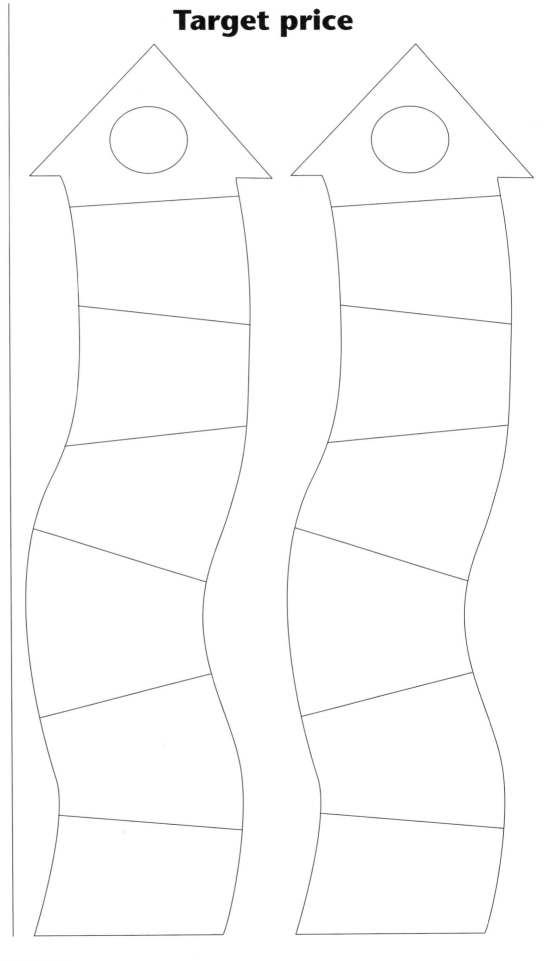

Spend £1

envelope
7p

stamp
25p

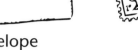

notepaper
8p/sheet

postcard
20p

birthday card
50p

pen
22p

Demonstrates that the child can add coin values to £1 and give change from £1, using coins.

Using and applying
- *Uses appropriate equipment (coins).*
- *Chooses and uses operations.*
- *Checks results.*

Give the child the sheet with some coins and base 10 apparatus. Ask her/him to complete the shopping lists, recording the total, price and the change from £1 in each case.

Note whether the child:
❑ finds totals accurately

works out change from:
❑ 50p
❑ £1

Teacher comments:

Shopping list

I envelope _____
I sheet of paper _____
I stamp _____

I spent _____
My change was _____

Shopping list

I birthday card _____
I stamp _____
I pen _____

I spent _____
My change was _____

Shopping list

2 stamps _____
I postcard _____
I pen _____

I spent _____
My change was _____

Shopping list

_____
_____
_____

I spent _____
My change was _____

Teachers' notes, page 35

NUMBER, MONEY & ALGEBRA

Demonstrates that the child can add amounts beyond £1 using coins, and record using decimal notation.

Using and applying
- *Uses appropriate equipment (coins).*
- *Checks own work with a calculator.*

Give the child the sheet, a calculator, coins and some base 10 apparatus. Ask her/him to write the prices on the shopping lists and add up the totals, then check the totals with a calculator and record their results.

Note whether the child:
❑ uses decimal notation correctly in recording
❑ adds totals above £1 accurately

Teacher comments:

Born to shop

crisps	banana	apple	snack bar	yoghurt
30p	18p	12p	25p	35p

Shopping list

2 packets of crisps ____

1 banana ____

2 snack bars ____

total ____

check [calculator] ▢▢▢▢

Shopping list

1 yoghurt ____

1 snack bar ____

2 bananas ____

total ____

check [calculator] ▢▢▢▢

Shopping list

2 apples ____

2 snack bars ____

2 yoghurts ____

total ____

check [calculator] ▢▢▢▢

Shopping list

____

____

____

____

total ____

check [calculator] ▢▢▢▢

Teachers' notes, pages 35–36

Demonstrates the child's ability to solve a money problem in a realistic context.

Using and applying
• Selects the mathematics for the task.
• Works in a realistic context.

Prepare the sheet by writing a mathematical problem in words at the top of each of the two panels (some examples are suggested in the Teachers' notes). Ask the child to answer the questions in the space provided. Make coins and/or base 10 apparatus available if the child requests them, but discourage the use of calculators.

Apparatus used:

Strategies applied:

Teacher comments:

Teachers' notes, page 36

Name

Date

Fruit corner

 15p

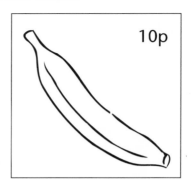 10p

30p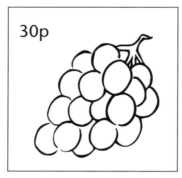

20p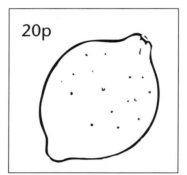

Name _____   *Date* _____

In its place

Demonstrates that the child can respond to oral descriptions of positions in an order, order the positions 1st to 6th and relate ordinal descriptions to each other.

Using and applying
• *Responds to oral questioning.*
• *Describes using mathematical language.*
• *Uses own recording.*

Help the child to label the pets according to their positions in the line, from 1st to 6th. Ask the child to answer the questions below, showing awareness of ordinal language. Finally, ask the child to draw, label and describe her/his own line of items, such as runners in a race or shoppers in a queue.

Note whether the child can use and respond appropriately to the ordinal numbers:

	use	respond
1st	❏	❏
2nd	❏	❏
3rd	❏	❏
4th	❏	❏
5th	❏	❏
6th	❏	❏

Teacher comments:

Where is the cat? _____

Which pet is 5th? _____

Where is the dog? _____

Where is the mouse? _____

Teachers' notes, page 36

Demonstrates the child's ability to make and describe a repeating pattern.

Using and applying
• *Works independently and selects her/his own materials.*
• *Makes predictions.*
• *Identifies and applies a general rule.*

Provide a collection of small items (for example, buttons or shapes) in a variety of sizes, shapes and colours. Ask the child to make a repeating pattern on the track, starting with the first space and putting one item only on each space, then record the pattern using crayons or pens. Tell her/him to look where particular items come in relation to their ordinal positions. Ask her/him to predict for the 10th, 15th and 20th spaces.

Note whether the child:
❑ can create a repeating pattern
❑ relates pattern to ordinal position
❑ predicts randomly
❑ predicts with reasoning

Teacher comments:

Name

Date

All in order

Name _____   *Date* _____

Round and round

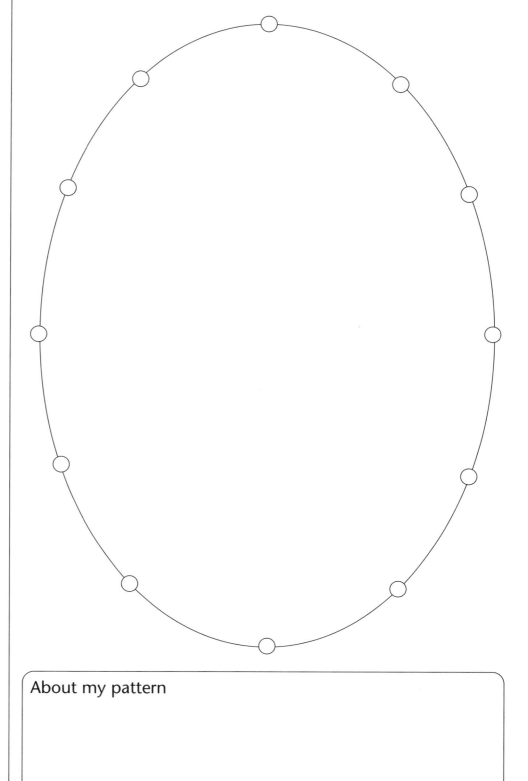

Demonstrates the child's ability to recognise and create a closed repeating pattern.

Using and applying
- *Selects materials for the task.*
- *Discusses the work.*

Provide a range of small items (such as counters or buttons) in different shapes, sizes and colours. Ask the child to place an item on each spot around the oval so as to make a closed repeating pattern. Discuss the completed pattern with the child. Scribe her/his comments in the box at the bottom of the page. Finally, let her/him record the pattern on the sheet by drawing and/or colouring.

Note whether the child:
❑ selects her/his own materials for the task
❑ identifies the unit of repeat
❑ appreciates the closed nature of the repeat

Teacher comments:

About my pattern

Teachers' notes, page 37

Demonstrates the child's ability to add pairs of consecutive numbers and identify a general rule.

Using and applying
- *Records her/his answers.*
- *Identifies a general rule.*

Ask the child to pick any pair of consecutive numbers from the number line on the sheet and add them together. Encourage him/her to select various different pairs of consecutive numbers and record their totals, looking for patterns in the results. If appropriate, ask the child to select examples above 10.

Note whether the child:
❏ calculates accurately
❏ records her/his work
❏ identifies a general rule
❏ provides an example outside the range 0–9
❏ uses practical apparatus
❏ uses no practical apparatus

Teacher comments:

Name _____   Date _____

Pick a pair

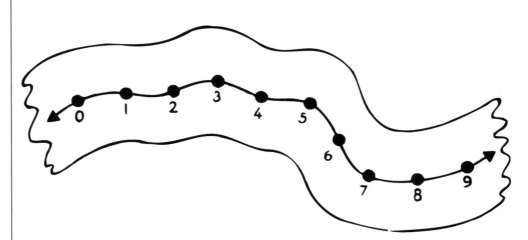

Record your work below.

What do you notice? _____

_____

_____

_____

Name   *Date*

Up and down

Demonstrates that the child can count forwards and backwards in steps of 2, 5 and 10.

Using and applying
• *Uses a number line accurately.*

Ask the child to work through the sheet, recording in the spaces provided. Have longer number lines available for the child to use. While the children are working on the sheet, ask individuals to count in 2s, 5s and 10s orally for you. Encourage them to comment on the patterns they have noticed.

Note whether the child can:
❑ count forwards in steps of 2, 5 and 10
❑ count backwards in steps of 2, 5 and 10
❑ count orally in 2s, 5s and 10s
❑ comment on the patterns arising

Teacher comments:

Start at 0. Count on in 2s.

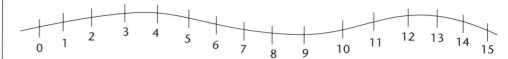

Start at 1. Count on in 2s.

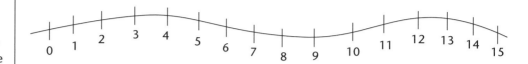

Start at 0. Count on in 5s. Write the numbers you land on here.

Start at 50. Count back in 5s.

Start at 100. Count back in 10s.

Start at 7. Count on in 10s.

Start at 114. Count on in 2s.

Teachers' notes, page 37

Demonstrates that the child can use different operations to complete a number chain. Demonstrates that the child can use a calculator to check mental calculations.

Using and applying
• *Selects mathematics for the task.*
• *Checks her/his work.*

Prepare the sheet (before copying) by writing the same number in the first and last circle. Give each child a copy of the sheet and a calculator. The task is to use any number operation to generate a sequence of numbers, for example:

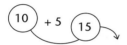

The sequence must begin and end with the number given. Encourage the child to use mental methods (or counting apparatus), and to use the calculator for checking only.

Note whether the child:
❑ uses the calculator to check
❑ works mentally
❑ uses counting apparatus

Teacher comments:

Teachers' notes, page 37

Name   *Date*

Number chains

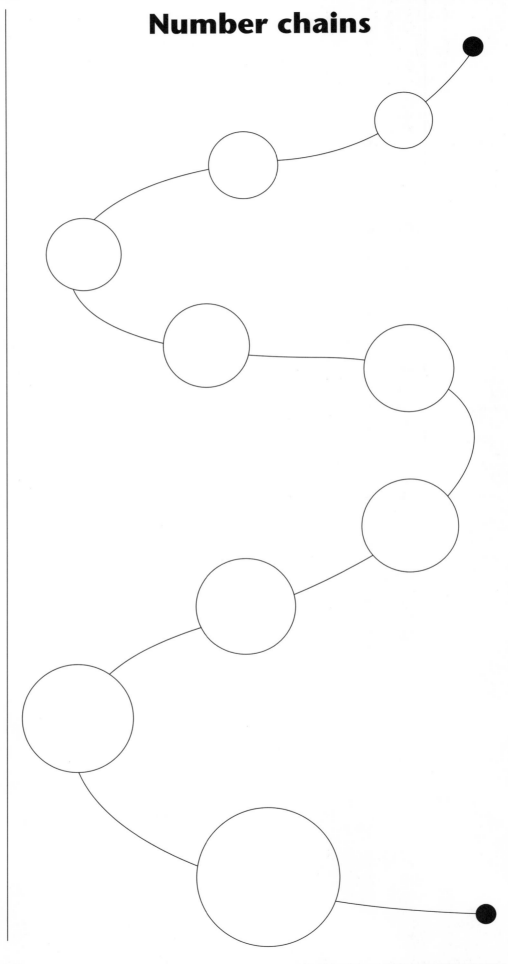

DATA HANDLING

DATA HANDLING

This introduction provides a background and rationale for the data handling activities in this chapter.

Data are facts which derive from the real world, but can be represented in a mathematical way. The assessment of data handling skills at Key Stage 1 needs to be placed within the wider context of work on Number. The children's ability to sort, record and present data should be related to their more general recording and communication skills in mathematics. Links can also be made with the children's developing ability to handle and interpret data from science investigations.

SORTING

Rules for sorting

The notion of a rule is fundamental to the process of sorting. This need not necessarily be driven by mathematical contexts: the act of sorting itself is inherently rule-driven. However, many circumstances lend themselves to mathematical rules: shapes of blocks, number of wheels on toys, and so on.

Two-way sorting

At different times, the child will need to generate criteria for sorting or to use given criteria. As the child becomes more aware of the properties of objects, he/she can be expected to sort a given set by more than one criterion – for example, sorting buttons by size and number of holes. This kind of work leads the child to use such forms of representation as the Carroll diagram, the tree diagram and the Venn diagram. In the context of two-way sorting, these forms are mathematically equivalent. (See Figure 1.)

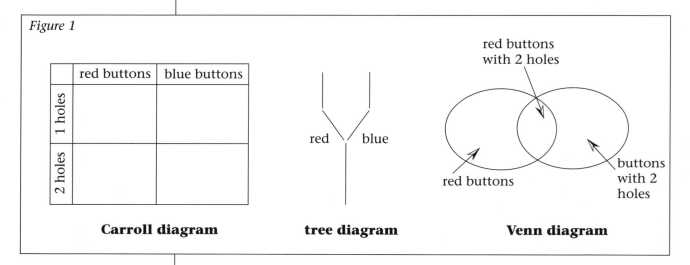

Figure 1

Carroll diagram   **tree diagram**   **Venn diagram**

MAPPING AND GRAPHICAL REPRESENTATION

Mapping

Mappings are a basic way of displaying relationships. Because of their clear link to practical contexts, mappings are often used as a stepping-stone to graphical methods of representation. When mappings show a one-to-many or many-to-one relationship (for example, when several children have a similar pet), this result might lend itself to representation in the form of a pictogram.

Graphical representation

Graphs involve a further level of abstraction in which objects are represented by a space measured on an adjacent linear scale. A block graph is typically used to represent discrete items of data: separate columns of information (for example, different pets) have values represented by their heights. A bar chart is typically used to display data of a more continuous nature; as such, the columns are typically represented together without spaces between them. The data may also feature fractional quantities, and the scale is therefore drawn in a way which is similar to a number line. With all forms of representation, it is important for the child to recognise that the presentation should match the needs of the audience, and to present the data in a clear and unambiguous way.

PROBLEM SOLVING

A data handling activity at Key Stage 1 might begin with a question that requires answering (for example, 'Where is there most litter in the school grounds?') This gives rise to a need to decide how the data are to be collected and the categories into which they might be grouped. The data then needs to be collected by a method that is efficient and suitably accurate. Decisions then need to be made about the most appropriate form of representation, based on the data and the anticipated audience. Finally, the results need to be reviewed and interpreted. Conclusions may be drawn that give rise to further questions for investigation. As teachers, we must make sure that the child has experience of all these different elements and does not, for example, assume that data handling ends when the representation is complete.

TOWARDS PROBABILITY

Probability is an aspect of mathematics which both relates to the collection of data and links with work on aspects of Number such as fractions and percentages. In Key Stage 1, awareness of probability will arise out of everyday situations (for example, 'Will it be a wet playtime?') At a later stage, the child will develop an awareness that probability can sometimes be ascribed a numerical value and that this value relates to the likelihood of that event happening. Work using items such as coins or dice allows an awareness of probability to develop through work on the relative frequencies of different outcomes.

TEACHING NOTES FOR INDIVIDUAL ACTIVITIES

Sorted!

page 96

Sorting according to a non-mathematical rule Before the task, allow time for the children to handle the greeting cards and talk about them. At this stage, you should avoid focusing on responses which will be appropriate for the assessment.

Criteria for sorting should allow clear division of the cards into two subsets. Suitable examples might include:
- cartoon/not cartoon;
- animals/not animals;
- birthday cards/not birthday cards;
- funny cards/not funny cards.

Encourage the child to think of several different ways of sorting.

Your assessment should focus on the extent to which the child can invent appropriate rules for sorting, and the accuracy of the subsequent sort. A child who is less confident in sorting will need a simple rule to be provided, such as those suggested above. An able child should offer several possible criteria for sorting without being prompted. In both cases, you should expect the sorting to be consistent and accurate.

Dominoes

page 97

Sorting according to a rule The child should have had some opportunity to use dominoes beforehand. This activity can be conducted with individuals or with a small group. You will need a standard (28-piece) set of dominoes.

There are several possible versions of this activity, and you may wish to tailor these to suit the child:

Task A – Provide a sorting ring and ask the child to use this to sort the dominoes which feature six or more spots in total.

Task B – Ask the child to sort according to a rule of her/his choice, then ask what the rule is (examples might be: doubles, fewer than 6 spots in total, an even number of spots, seven spots, the two halves have a difference of one).

Task C – Carry out the sort for yourself and ask the child to say what your rule is.

You may need to annotate the sheet briefly to record the extent of support and direction given. The assessment checklist focuses on the level of independence and the mathematical vocabulary used in sorting. A child in the early stages of sorting may find it difficult to come up with a rule of her/his own. In such cases, you might expect the child to follow a simple rule that you have provided (for example, 'Find all the dominoes with just five spots in total'). A confident child may sort in several ways and begin to identify mathematical significance in some of the sorts (for example, 'These all have six spots. They're like add sums – five and one, four and two...').

The task in which the child must establish another person's rule for sorting is the most challenging. This calls for considerable mental agility and a broad base of mathematical knowledge and vocabulary. The three tasks represent a progression in difficulty. You may elect to take the child through this progression, or alternatively to select one activity that most closely matches the child's prior attainment.

Sisters and brothers
page 98

Using a mapping diagram Some previous experience of one-to-one, one-to-many and many-to-one mappings is important for this task. The activity could be carried out with a smaller group than six children. The children are collecting data as a group, but recording and commenting on the results individually. Figure 2 shows an example of a complete mapping.

A younger or less able child may be unable to provide an appropriate comment, or may just make a statement relating to one child (for example, 'Fred has two brothers and sisters.') An older or more able child may refer to features of mathematical significance, such as 'I noticed that two people have got one brother or sister.' The most able child may be able to interpret the diagram in order to answer a direct question such as 'How many brothers and sisters are there altogether?' Some children may wish to record half-brothers or half-sisters in a separate way; others may be happy to use the given categories without alteration.

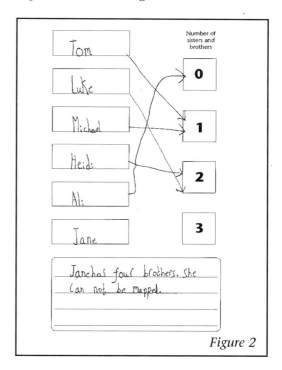

Figure 2

Not this, not that
page 99

Using negation in sorting You should have explored the notation of 'not...' with the children as part of a discussion. This language, known as negation, is a vital part of later work on sorting (for example, when working with Carroll diagrams involving two pairs of criteria). A variation of 'Twenty Questions' would help to reinforce this area in a fun and purposeful way:

T: I'm thinking of a number fewer than one hundred.
C: Is it even?
T: No, it is not even.
C: Is it greater than fifty?
T: No, it is not greater than fifty.
C: Is it more than twenty-five? ... and so on.

For the task on this sheet, some preliminary work on shape (and associated vocabulary) is essential. The kind of sorting criteria which the child should suggest might include:

- names of shapes (as in 'not a hexagon');
- number of sides (as in 'not four sides');
- straight/curved sides (as in 'not straight sides');
- angles (as in 'not right-angled corners').

If the child has insufficient knowledge of shape, you may opt to modify the sheet by replacing the shape outlines with numbers. For example, the number 7 could be described as 'Not more than 10', 'Not an even number', 'Not fewer than 5' and 'Not in the 5 times table'.

The assessment will inform your judgement of the child's level of understanding in the chosen area of content. The shape task, for example, will reveal the extent to which the child knows a shape by its properties. You may need to encourage the child to think of a diversity of responses, not to stay within a narrow range of sorting criteria.

Double sort

page 100

Sorting on a Venn diagram The intersection of sets needs to have been encountered at an earlier stage. It could be explored by sorting with two discrete rings and then discussing where to place an object which rightly belongs in both sets. If physical sorting rings are used, they can be drawn together and made to overlap.

If the child is not familiar with the numerical ideas in this task, the sorting criteria can be changed to allow easier access. For example:
• shapes of various types and colours, with tags labelled 'red' and 'triangle';
• a range of materials, with tags labelled 'waterproof' and 'natural'.

The assessment checklist offers a brief summary of some of the key objectives. You may need to add further notes if support or extension is needed. The task of following the conventions of a Venn diagram is a challenging one; if difficulties arise you should provide opportunities in other contexts, in order to ascertain whether the problem is created by the content demands of the task or by the conventions of the diagram.

Sorting tree

page 101

Using a basic tree diagram The child should have had previous experience of sorting with a range of natural and artificial materials. An appropriate theme for sorting in this task might involve work in another subject area. For some children, you may elect to draw the objects for sorting prior to getting started. The rule for sorting should generate two criteria, with one the negation of the other (for example, 'can fly/cannot fly).

A younger or less able child may need support throughout this task, and may be unable to establish suitable statements for sorting. Such a child may also find it difficult to recognise that the two options must cover all eventualities (for example, 'can fly/cannot fly'), and may therefore select two headings (such as 'can fly/has no legs') which are not strictly complementary. An older or more able child will be able to think of further objects for sorting, and may even consider additional statements to branch a further stage. Both of the two branches, for example, could be split (using the same rule) to form a total of four subsets. The rule for the second sort could be 'has legs/no legs', for example. The more able child should consider suitable objects to extend the sort in this way, and should use the sorting criteria effectively to negotiate through the tree diagram.

Best of three
page 102

Collecting and representing information This task can be managed as a group activity involving several (four to eight) children. The task is relatively open, and the level of support required will not become apparent until the children engage in the task. Allow each child to select a set of options: favourite crisps, drinks, school subjects, and so on. Restricting the number of options to three helps to make it easier to draw conclusions from the data. Stress the importance of making the data understandable for others; but try not to specify the nature of the presentation. At the end, as well as asking the child to comment on the data, you might ask specific questions (for example, 'How many more preferred... than...?') to identify whether the child can use and apply mathematical information presented in the form that he/she has chosen.

Unless they have had some previous experience of recording graphically, most children will use a pictorial representation. (Figure 3 shows an example of each method.) Whatever form of representation they use, you should consider how confidently they apply themselves and the extent to which the end product communicates the information clearly. An able child may use tally marks as part of the data collection process. He/she should provide an appropriate statement and be able to answer direct questions such as 'How many children chose either ... or ...?'

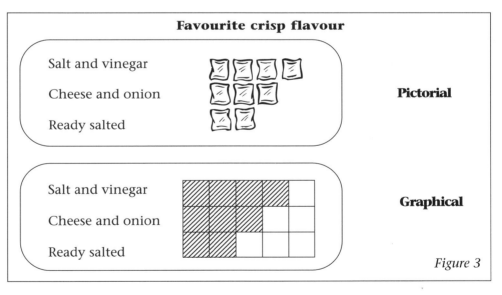

Figure 3

Our favourite colour
page 103

Interpreting information from a bar chart This task requires the child to interpret information which has already been collected in a class activity. When collecting the data, make sure that each child appreciates the need to 'vote' only once. Display the data on a board using words and numbers only (for example, 'red 10').

The questions to be written on the sheet could be adapted and selected from the following list (in increasing order of difficulty):
• Which colour do you like best?
• Which was the class's favourite colour?
• How many colours did we choose from?

- How many people liked green?
- How many more children liked blue than yellow?
- How many fewer children liked blue than red?
- How many children chose either red or yellow?
- How many children voted altogether?

The assessment focus is how well the child is able to interpret the charts in answering the questions. The checklist on the sheet suggests some indicators of performance. Further differentiation depends on the complexity of the questions asked.

What's the difference?
page 104

Gather and interpret data involving probability The child will need to have undertaken some work on finding differences between numbers. It would also be useful for the child to have some experience relating to the notion of probability (for example, in the context of dice games).

The assessment of this task relates to the mathematics involved, the representation of the results and their subsequent interpretation. A younger or less able child may not have had sufficient experience of probability to become aware that the six possible outcomes are not equally likely. For such a child, the task will be challenging in terms of the calculation and representation of the results. An older or more able child may come to appreciate that some differences occur more frequently than others, and begin to understand why. The most able child may attempt to list all the possible combinations, and use these findings as a means to explain the results. Figure 4 shows all the possible combinations. Note that, for example, a difference of 5 can only be made in two ways, whereas a difference of 1 can be made in ten ways.

Figure 4

diff.	1	2	3	4	5	6
1	0	1	2	3	4	5
2	1	0	1	2	3	4
3	2	1	0	1	2	3
4	3	2	1	0	1	2
5	4	3	2	1	0	1
6	5	4	3	2	1	0

Databases
page 105

Using a computer database Several versions are available for use in primary schools (including *Ourfacts* and *Dataease*), and so the sheet has been left open-ended. The choice of theme is also unspecified by the sheet. For simplicity, you may opt for information structured according to Yes/No responses. Figure 5 shows an example.

Use the assessment checklist on the sheet to identify strengths and weaknesses, and to detail competencies. The least experienced computer user will need to be shown how to type information into the computer, and will be unfamiliar with keyboard facilities (such as the Return/Enter key). A more independent learner will enter information and save it for later reference. Such a child may also interrogate the data by asking (for example) for a list of people with one or more pets. The most able child will use all the available facilities, including asking questions such as 'Which people have a brother and a sister?' You should question the child about the information he/she has found, in order to assess her/his ability to interpret and comment on it.

> Name of child:
>
> Pets?   Yes/No
>
> Bicycle?   Yes/No
>
> Brother?   Yes/No
>
> Sister?   Yes/No

Figure 5

Making a graph page 106

If possible, choose a computer program that will allow the child some choice in the style of presentation which he/she can then justify to you. This might be a bar chart or pie chart, or in the order 0 → 7, or in the order of the number of teeth lost (for example: 5 6/7/1 0 3 4 2).

When discussing the chart with the child, it will be important to include:
• Questions about using the programme – choice of presentation style, entering the information, trying out different ways on screen.
• Questions about the information itself – how many children have lost the most teeth? How many children have lost three teeth? How many more children have lost three teeth than one tooth? How many children are in the class altogether?

In the child's answer to the first question on the sheet, look for selection of important or general facts (for example, the fact that most of the children lost two, three or four teeth, or that the most common number of teeth lost was two) rather than randomly selected facts such as that no children lost five teeth. In the child's answer to the final question on the sheet, look for awareness that most of the children will have lost more teeth; this shows an ability to connect the data on the sheet with general knowledge about children in this age group.

Name

Date

Sorted!

*Demonstrates the child's
ability to sort according to
a non-mathematical rule.*

Using and applying
- *Talks about the work.*
- *Records findings.*

Provide ten greeting cards
and ask the child to sort
them according to a rule
of her/his choice. Suggest
a suitable rule if necessary.
Then ask the child to sort
by another rule.
Encourage the child to
think of further sorting
criteria. Finally, he/she can
stick one of the cards on
to the sheet to exemplify
one of the sorting criteria.

Note whether the child:
❑ sorts by a given rule
❑ sorts by her/his own
rule
❑ sorts consistently

Teacher comments:

My rule:

Teachers' notes, page 90

Name

Date

Dominoes

Demonstrates the child's ability to sort according to a mathematical rule.

Using and applying
• *Talks about her/his work.*
• *Records in pictorial form.*

Provide a standard set of 28 dominoes and ask the child to sort them according to either a given rule or one of her/his own (see Teachers' notes). When the sort is finished, ask the child to record some examples on the sheet.

Note whether the child:
❑ sorts by a provided rule
❑ sorts by her/his own rule

Mathematical vocabulary used:

Teacher comments:

✓

✗

The rule is: _____

_____

Teachers' notes, pages 90–91

Name _____   *Date* _____

Sisters and brothers

Demonstrates the child's ability to use a mapping diagram.

Using and applying
• *Uses mapping to record information.*
• *Interprets the information presented.*
• *Makes predictions based on experience.*

Provide a group of six children with one copy each of the sheet. Ask them to predict what number of brothers and sisters will be the most common in their group. Explain or demonstrate how to start the diagram by writing in a name and mapping it to the appropriate number using an arrow. Leave the group to complete the task. Finally, ask them a question (or elicit a statement) about the results; each child should record a comment or answer at the bottom of the sheet.

Note whether the child:
❑ makes a prediction
❑ works accurately
❑ answers a question
❑ provides a statement

Teacher comments:

Number of sisters and brothers

0

1

2

3

Teachers' notes, page 91

Name _____

Date _____

Not this, not that

*Demonstrates the child's
ability to use negation.*

Using and applying
• *Selects the mathematics
for the task.*
• *Talks about the work.*

Ask the child to colour in
the three shapes on the
sheet. This will give one
property for sorting (for
example, 'not red').
Encourage the child to
think of two further
properties of a
mathematical nature for
each shape (for example,
'not triangle' or 'not with
right-angled corners').
Encourage individuals in
the group to share their
ideas afterwards.

Note whether the child:
❏ can use negation
❏ can apply
mathematical criteria

Teacher comments:

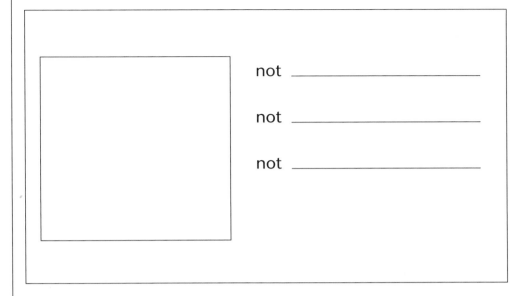

not _____

not _____

not _____

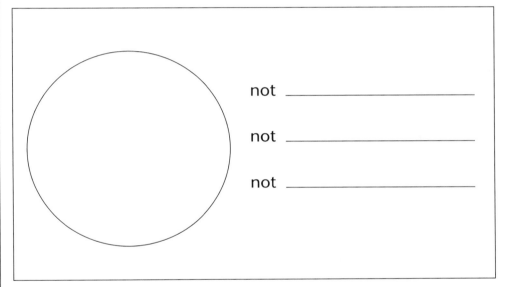

not _____

not _____

not _____

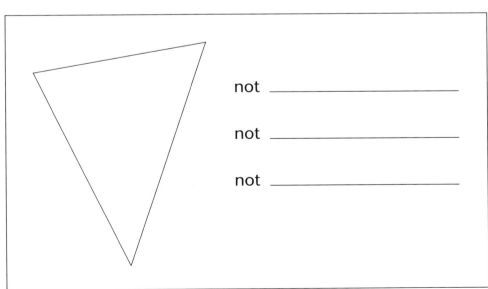

not _____

not _____

not _____

Teachers' notes, pages
91–92

Name   Date

Double sort

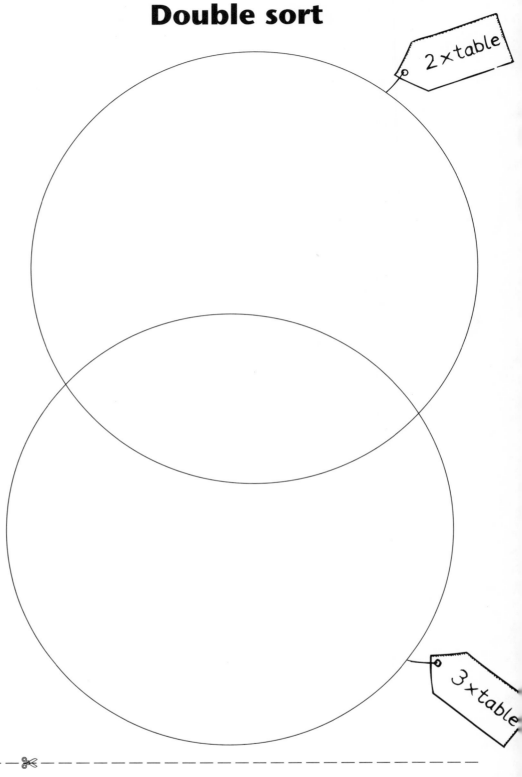

Demonstrates the child's ability to sort using a Venn diagram.

Using and applying
• *Selects the mathematics for the task.*
• *Records diagrammatically.*
• *Makes predictions.*

Ask the child to cut out the numerals and stick them onto the Venn diagram, according to the sorting criteria. (If appropriate, help the child by placing one of the numerals and explaining why it belongs there.) Discuss the answer(s) in the overlap: can the child predict what other numbers (between 10 and 20) might go there? Encourage her/him to write two more numbers on the blank squares and stick these onto the sheet.

Note whether the child:
❑ can sort using double criteria
❑ recognises odd/even numbers
❑ can predict for the numbers 10–20

Teacher comments:

Teachers' notes, page 92

3	4	2	6	8
9	1	7		

Name

Date

Sorting tree

Demonstrates the child's ability to sort using a basic tree diagram.

Using and applying
• *Records diagrammatically.*
• *Follows the instructions given.*

Ask the child to draw five objects on a given theme in the boxes at the bottom of this sheet (for example, minibeasts). Either suggest or ask the child to invent a rule for sorting. Ask her/him to write the categories on the branches (for example, 'wings' and 'no wings').

Now ask the child to sort the objects appropriately and stick her/his drawings onto the tree. Finally, encourage the child to suggest a further theme, then provide her/him with appropriate objects for sorting.

Note whether the child:
❑ sorts by a provided rule
❑ sorts by her/his own rule
❑ follows instructions successfully

Teacher comments:

Teachers' notes, pages 92–93

Name   *Date*

Best of three

Demonstrates the child's
ability to collect and
represent information.

Using and applying
• *Works methodically.*
• *Communicates the
information.*
• *Selects a mathematical
form of presentation.*

Ask the child to collect
information from the
group about their
favourite of three options
(for example, crisp
flavours or pop groups).
The sheet should be used
to gather the information
and to display it for others
to read. Ask the child to
represent the information
in any way he/she thinks
is appropriate. Finally,
discuss the results and ask
the child to write a
comment on them at the
bottom of the sheet.

Note whether the child:
❑ represents the data
accurately
❑ represents the data
appropriately
❑ works confidently

Teacher comments:

About the results:

Teachers' notes, page 93

Name   *Date*

Our favourite colour

Red

Green

Blue

Yellow

1 2 3 4 5 6 7 8 9 10 11 12

Demonstrates the child's ability to interpret information from a bar chart.

Using and applying
• **Selects the mathematics for the task.**
• **Records data graphically.**

Collect class data on favourite colours, offering the four options given on the sheet. Prepare the sheet by writing five questions appropriate to the ability of individuals and/or groups in the class (see Teachers' notes for suggestions). Tell the child to record the data on the chart at the top of the sheet by colouring in the appropriate boxes. Then read the questions aloud and record the child's answers, or let the child work on these independently.

Note whether the child:
❑ records accurately
❑ interprets the chart correctly
❑ talks about her/his work

Teacher comments:

Teachers' notes, pages 93–94

DATA HANDLING

Demonstrates the child's ability to gather and interpret data (involving probability).

Using and applying
• *Makes predictions and gives reasons.*
• *Records using a diagram.*
• *Talks about her/his results.*

Provide the child (or group) with two dice. Demonstrate how to calculate the differences between two dice throws, and show the child how to record this information on the chart. Ask the child which column he/she thinks will be filled first if the dice are thrown many times and the differences recorded. Ask her/him to explain or justify the prediction. Then leave her/him to test the prediction. When one column has been filled, ask the child what has been found out. Scribe the child's response, or let her/him record it, at the bottom of the sheet.

Note whether the child:
❑ predicts with reasons
❑ records accurately
❑ interprets the results

Teacher comments:

What's the difference?

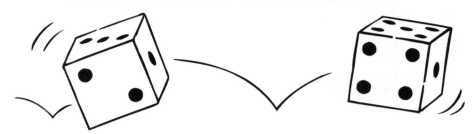

Find the difference and record it on the chart below.

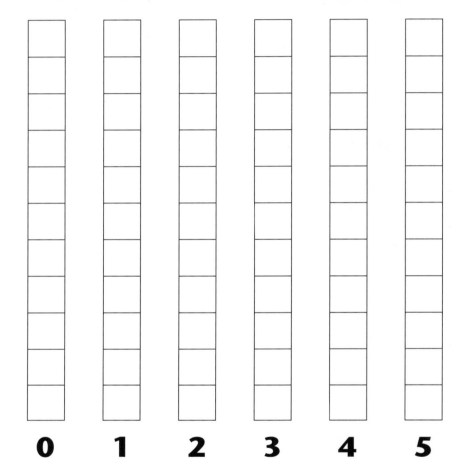

0   1   2   3   4   5

What I found:

_____

_____

_____

DATA HANDLING

Databases

Demonstrates the child's ability to use a computer database.

Using and applying
• *Uses IT in mathematics.*
• *Asks and responds to questions.*

Allow the child to work independently to complete the sheet, before and after working on a computer database. The sheet is open-ended, to suit a range of simple databases available for use on the computer. Use the checklist below to detail the child's skills, noting the level (and nature) of support given. Ask the child some questions about the data he/she has presented.

Note whether the child:
❑ enters information
❑ saves information
❑ loads the file (if working over more than one session)
❑ prints
❑ asks a question (one heading)
❑ asks a question (two headings)
Level of support:

Teacher comments:

Our database is about _____

It has _____ entries.

I asked this question:

This is a printout of my results:

Name   Date

Making a graph

The children in Class 1 found out how many of their teeth had come out. This is what they found:

0	teeth	4
1	tooth	2
2	teeth	8
3	teeth	5
4	teeth	7
5	teeth	0
6	teeth	2
7	teeth	2

Use   to make a graph of the results.

Clip it to this sheet.

What does your graph tell you about the children in Class 1?

_____

_____

_____

_____

What would you expect them to find if they collected this information again next year?

_____

_____

_____

SHAPE & SPACE

*Vocabulary of shape
and space*

SHAPE AND SPACE

This chapter presents activities to assess the child's command of the language and properties of two- and three-dimensional shapes, positional language and movement around routes. The activities will give you opportunities to observe the child working practically with shapes, positions and locations, and to talk with the child during and/or after the task to pick up on points you have noticed, ask questions and evaluate the child's use of appropriate mathematical language in this context.

In this area, the child's use of language is particularly important. There are several aspects to this:
• specific shape names (triangle, cuboid);
• words to describe the properties of shapes (curved, right angle, symmetry, straight);
• words to describe how shapes relate to each other (repeating pattern, tessellate);
• words to describe where things are in relation to each other (next to, to the right of, behind);
• words to describe movement and turn (forward, quarter turn to the right).

Because of the complexity of this language, the teacher's role in listening to how the child uses language with peers in the activity, and in questioning the child after the activity, is particularly important.

PRIOR KNOWLEDGE AND EXPERIENCE

This area of mathematics is one in which the child may have accumulated quite a lot of prior knowledge, language and understanding. The child may have encountered 2D and 3D shapes through building with blocks and construction kits or cutting and sticking with paper and sticky shapes. He/she may have explored the effect of turning shapes when working on a jigsaw and manipulating the pieces; and may have tried various routes when playing with toy cars on a play mat or around obstacles on the floor. Many children will have listened to and used positional language throughout their daily life in order to find things and orient themselves.

When the child is presented with more formal and structured tasks, it is important that her/his prior experience is taken into account. Some of these tasks may assess what is already known, allowing the teacher to work from this in planning to fill gaps and move the child forward. In particular, the teacher may check that the child is using language correctly. The child may know the right 'shape words' to use, for example, but not exactly which shape to apply a particular word to.

*Assessment through
observation*

METHODS AND STRATEGIES

The practical nature of this area of mathematics and the strong possibility of an existing basis on which to build make it essential for the teacher to observe the child working on the task, and to question the child during and after the task. Another important aspect of these assessments is that they give the teacher the opportunity to observe how the child *approaches* the task, in addition to her/his knowledge and understanding. Those tasks which involve a stronger element of investigation can be used to assess the child's method of organisation, and how the child uses what he/she has found out to answer the challenge set or to make a generalisation.

Visible methods

While quite a lot of number investigation is internal and difficult to observe, the work of manipulating and building with shapes, exploring routes and turns and testing for symmetry and tessellation is likely to involve the child in doing things that the teacher can see clearly. It may thus be directly visible when a child works through a sequence of shapes methodically, noting findings as he/she goes along; or when a child works with shapes as they come to hand, more or less randomly, and then tries to remember what happened.

TEACHING NOTES FOR INDIVIDUAL ACTIVITIES

*Flat shapes

page 118*

Recognising and drawing 2D shapes After the child has named the shapes orally, recording can be completed in the form most appropriate to the child. In the early stages, a child might stick down the shape labels. A child with more developed writing skills might write the name of each shape emergently, or copy from the label.

In the second part of the task, specify which shape is to be drawn in each space. The child may wish to draw each shape a few times to arrive at one he/she is satisfied with. He/she might also comment on the shapes descriptively. These responses should be noted, especially if they demonstrate correct use of mathematical language (terms such as *curved, straight, corner, side*). Children who are confident about the properties of these flat shapes and experienced in drawing them (both around 3D shapes/with stencils and freehand) should be able to draw the shapes recognisably. Children's comments on their work might reveal understanding of the properties of the shapes, even if their drawings are not fully developed.

*More 2D shapes

page 119*

Recognising and drawing 2D shapes In the first part of the task, the child can either stick down the labels or copy from them, as appropriate. In the second part of the task, the child should draw the shapes freehand. He/she might wish to try several drawings before arriving at one that he/she is satisfied with. Alternatively, he/she might draw several different versions which are all correct, though they are not all regular. A child with more experience of shapes and their properties will be aware that a hexagon is a six-sided shape which does not have to look like the one on the sheet. A child at an earlier stage will try to reproduce the usual regular hexagon he/she is used to. The assessment can be extended by asking the child to describe these shapes using mathematical terms (*sides, corners, curved, straight*).

*My first tangram

page 120*

Manipulating and describing shapes Scribe the child's comments onto the sheet. Children are likely to describe the shapes and arrangements they have made by relating them to known objects such as boats, trees and stars. Children who are more confident with mathematical language can be prompted to spot and name regular shapes that they can see within their work. Children who understand the properties of shapes should also be able to point out and explain shapes which only look different because of their orientation. Figure 1 shows some typical shapes/patterns and children's comments.

Figure 1

'I used my 4 triangles to make a large and small square.'

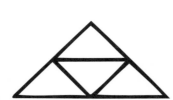

'I made a bigger triangle.'

'I made a Christmas tree.'

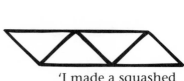

'I made a squashed rectangle.'

Short straw, long straw
page 121

Making and recognising triangles of different types The use of two different-coloured sets of straws is recommended for this, because it will help to distinguish the two types of straw and will make recording easier. The shorter straw should be approximately two-thirds the length of the longer straw (7cm and 10cm lengths are ideal).

The child may be surprised to find that only four different triangles can be made (see Figure 2). If possible, simplify the recording by providing coloured pencils which correspond to the two straw colours. In some instances, you may need to record on the child's behalf.

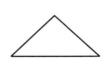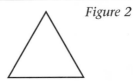

Figure 2

Encourage the child to examine the triangles and to talk about their properties. The child may comment on the **similarity** (see definition below) of the two equilateral triangles, and may recognise the fact that the other two shapes (isosceles triangles) are made from two straws of one size and one straw of the other size. Ask the child whether all the triangles have been found, and encourage her/him to give you a convincing reason why or why not. The child will not necessarily find all four solutions, and may simply remark that the triangles are different. It may not be appreciated that a triangle which is simply a rotation of another arrangement is essentially the same triangle. A child with an extended awareness of and confidence in shape will use specific mathematical vocabulary to describe the properties of, and the differences between, the various shapes. A logical comment may draw attention to the pairs of equilateral and isosceles triangles, though the child may not know these terms.

*Two shapes are **similar** if they share the same mathematical properties except for size: one is an enlarged version of the other.*

What's my rule?

page 122

Sorting shapes according to a rule You will need to provide a set of 2D and/or 3D shapes, with scope for sorting in a number of different ways. A selection containing both regular and irregular shapes will allow a diversity of responses. For this reason you may need to prepare your own set of cut-outs (such as those shown in Figure 3), since many commercial materials tend to favour regular representations of shapes.

Figure 3

The two different versions of this task could both be used, perhaps taking turns; or only one version could be used. If you invent a rule for sorting, appropriate possibilities might be:
- straight sides/not straight sides;
- curved sides/not curved sides;
- both straight and curved sides/either straight or curved sides but not both;
- more than four sides/four sides or less;
- more than one line of symmetry/not more than one line of symmetry.

The assessment checklist on the sheet refers simply to the two different versions of the task. There is also a space to note words used by the child that relate to the names and/or properties of the shapes. The young child may initially sort by non-mathematical criteria (for example, 'shapes I like'). You may need to steer the discussion towards mathematical criteria, and to establish whether the rule can be described using appropriate mathematical vocabulary. A more able child may create several rules for sorting, and recognise the rule in a sort which is presented by the teacher. Such a child will work confidently with 3D shapes and use associated vocabulary to describe their properties.

Is it half?

page 123

Creating and recognising half of a given shape Although it is not essential to provide geoboards (or equivalent) for this task, they are recommended. Alternatively, you could provide an enlarged drawing square with a length of string to place on it, allowing for experimentation.

In presenting the example, you may want to ask: 'How do I know the shape has been halved?' The discussion could then focus on the notion of halves as two identical pieces and/or two shapes of equal area. Some children may still believe in the false notion of a 'big' and a 'little' half. Whatever the response, make a point of encouraging the routine strategy of checking.

For many children, the act of dividing the square into two identical sections will provide sufficient challenge. Able children may ask whether they can halve the square in ways that generate dissimilar shapes, and this should then be encouraged. Assess the child's knowledge of geometrical terms such as 'straight' and 'bent' (or 'broken'), and see whether the child routinely checks her/his work. Some possible answers are shown in Figure 4.

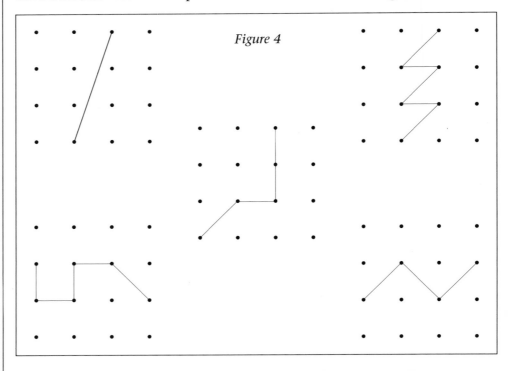

Figure 4

3D shape names

page 124

3D shapes: cube, cuboid, cone, cylinder, sphere and pyramid
Organise the working area so that after talking to you individually, the children can work in pairs with a screen between them so they can talk to each other but not see each other's shapes. Each child has the same set of shapes. The aim is for one child to describe a shape without naming it, and for the other to listen and pick out the correct shape. The task will need to be organised in such a way that you can listen to the mathematical language being used and record it on the sheet. This could make a useful contribution to assessing Speaking and Listening ability in a mathematical context.

Some children might use imprecise or irrelevant language, or make comparisons with known objects ('It's like a ...'). Children with a better grasp of mathematical language will be able to use words such as *corners*, *sides*, *edges*, *flat*, *straight*, *curved*, *faces*. Children who understand these terms may need little accurate description before they can work out which shape is being described.

Does it roll? Does it build?

page 125

Properties of 3D shapes While the child is working on this task, you will have an opportunity to observe her/his organisational skills in the context of an investigation, as well as her/his knowledge and understanding of the properties of 3D shapes. While investigating, some children may start to 'play' with the shapes and need prompting to return them to the task in hand. Other children may work purposefully, sorting or labelling the shapes according to their findings. A more able child might predict first and then go on to check with practical apparatus.

When talking about their findings and recording them, some children will describe their findings using the basic vocabulary of observation and will need your prompting to make generalisations linked to the properties of the shapes. A more experienced child will be able to generalise about the findings: 'Shapes with curved faces roll, shapes with flat faces slide' or 'Shapes with flat faces are best for building towers'.

Children can be challenged to extend their investigations, for example in rolling: 'Do shapes with curved faces all roll in the same way?' and in building: 'What about shapes with both flat and curved faces? What about shapes with a point at the top?'

Making boxes
page 126

3D shape nets and 2D faces Before undertaking this task, the child will need to have experience of the three 3D shapes involved. The child might draw the pieces used or write a list of their mathematical names. While the child is working, you should be able to observe whether he/she can visualise the shape and select appropriate pieces, or does not have a mental image of the shape and is experimenting by joining different pieces until the right one comes up. A child who is familiar with 3D shapes from construction work, and from looking at and describing shapes in her/his environment, will have a clearer idea of what he/she is aiming for.

Boxed in
page 127

Visualising 3D shapes and making nets The use of commercial plane shapes which interlock is highly recommended here, as they allow for rapid disassembly. Some children will find the recording problematic; in these cases, you may prefer to record the nets the children make on their behalf. Figure 5 shows the two solutions which are possible.

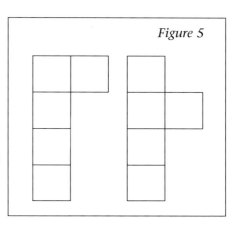
Figure 5

Through observation, you should attempt to judge whether successful nets are being arrived at by chance or whether a methodical approach is being employed. Some children, for example, may keep all but one piece of a successful net, and try to create new ones by moving the 'floating' piece around the perimeter to new locations. If the child works and records independently, you should briefly annotate words to that effect.

Symmetrical or not?
page 128

Figure 6

Explain the task using terms that the child is familiar with from her/his previous experience of symmetry. For example, if the term 'mirror line' has been used previously, replace 'line of symmetry' with this.

A child with a basic understanding of symmetry may note the symmetrical shapes. A greater understanding might be needed to recognise shapes with several lines of symmetry and to mark these on the shapes. A useful prompt to help the child draw a line of symmetry is asking the child to find the line of symmetry using a mirror and then to draw along it. Figure 6 shows the lines of symmetry which could be drawn on the shapes.

Mirror image

page 129

Recognising and creating shapes with reflective symmetry This task could be attempted by the individual child, or by pairs working in competition to make as many different symmetrical shapes as possible. All the pieces should be in contact (ie a single shape, not a pattern).

The assessment checklist on the sheet serves to differentiate responses to the task. In the case (see Figure 7) where a shape recorded by the child has no line symmetry but possesses rotational symmetry, you should note this on the checklist if you judge that the child has appreciated the notion of rotation. The shape shown in Figure 7 has rotational symmetry, since it appears the same when it has been rotated about the centre through 180 degrees.

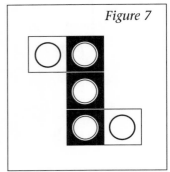

Figure 7

Fitting together

page 130

Tessellation The first part of the task gives the child an opportunity to investigate how regular 2D shapes tessellate before investigating further. The child should be able to demonstrate and explain what the word 'tessellate' means, and may be able to generalise about shapes that do and do not tessellate. If the child finds this section too difficult, you may wish to return to the second section at a later date. Watching the child work on the second part of the task will give you an opportunity to assess her/his ability to try different methods, check her/his work and work to a specific task. Figure 8 shows some possible combinations of two regular shapes that will tessellate.

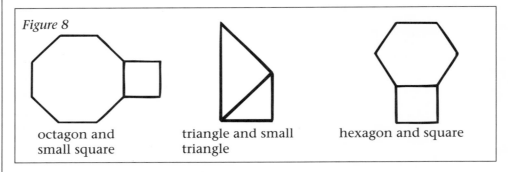

Figure 8

octagon and small square

triangle and small triangle

hexagon and square

Looking around

page 131

Tessellation When you send the child to look for patterns, make sure you have checked that there is a variety of tessellations in the area you are expecting the child to explore. If there are not enough different patterns, you should 'plant' some pieces of fabric, tiles, pictures, and so on. You may wish to write a location in each box (such as 'in the hall', 'in the cloakroom', 'in the library') to make sure that the child does not restrict her/his recording to brick patterns.

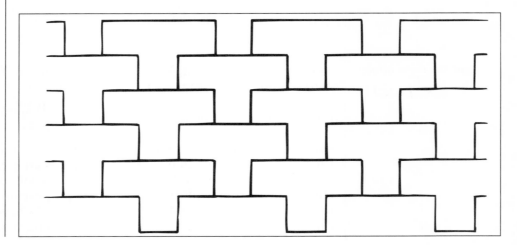

Repeating pattern This assessment is suitable for use with children at the beginning of Key Stage 1, who may be unable to read. Children who are at an early stage of understanding the nature of repeating patterns will find patterns with more elements difficult. Their own patterns will use only two or three elements, repeated in a straightforward way. Children with a more sophisticated understanding can be encouraged to make more complex patterns.

Positional language Work in gymnastics could provide an appropriate context for this task. Starting the task with all the children facing the same way will help to prevent confusion arising. The task can be differentiated by the difficulty and number of instructions given to each child. For example, a simple instruction might be 'James, sit in front of Mary'. A more demanding instruction might be 'Jinal, sit on the left of Kelly'; and an instruction requiring still more understanding might be 'Jasmin, sit behind and to the right of Mark'.

The children's descriptions of their own positions will help you to assess their understanding of and ability to use positional language. A child might start by describing one relationship, for example 'I am in front of Mark.' He/she might go on to use words such as *left* and *right* correctly. A more confident child might be able to describe her/his position in relation to all the fixed points available.

If you normally have bilingual support, you might carry out part or all of this task in the child's first language in order to assess the child's understanding of the terms themselves.

Recognising right angles If appropriate, the child could cut off the marked corner using safety scissors. Encourage the child to explore a wide range of objects and situations, such as door openings, books, posters, furniture and construction kit pieces.

Children who are less confident will measure with the card right angle each time, and may choose to measure items which are clearly not right angles. Children who understand what a right angle is will look for them and then check. Their search will thus appear more purposeful. In the child's recording, look for generalisations such as 'Books have four right angles' or 'I can change the opening of the door to make a right angle'.

Turning

page 135

The first part of the task assesses the child's ability to predict the outcome of turning a tile through a given number of quarter-turns. If a programmable toy is available, the child should check her/his prediction by attaching the pictorial tile to the toy and then making the toy move. The second part of the task assesses the child's ability to work out an instruction from a given start and end. Again, checking with a programmable toy would be a useful part of the task.

Children who can respond to turning instructions with understanding will be able to visualise and predict confidently. They will be able to generalise – for example, by telling you that two turns in either direction will have the same result or that four turns will bring you back to the start. Children at an early stage of understanding of this idea will rely heavily on turning their tiles, and might make mistakes in their turning and recording.

A possible extension to this activity would be to ask the child to explore a series of complete turns, each made up of four quarter-turns. Investigating this will give the child an opportunity to explore the four times table.

Gaps in the hedge

page 136

Using networks and working systematically If possible, the child should find all six combinations based on the three initial gaps and two final gaps. The stipulation that the route can pass through two gaps only is designed to prevent the child from complicating the task by weaving in and out of the gaps. The final question assesses the child's ability to extrapolate and generalise from a relatively simple to a more complex network.

The principal focus of this assessment is the child's ability to work independently in the context of a spatial challenge. To this end, you should talk to the child in order to ascertain her/his responses to the questions. A younger or less able child may find some examples of routes through the network. An older child may work more systematically through the task, explaining how he/she knows that all the possibilities have been accounted for. An able child may explicitly relate the number of gaps in each of the barriers to the resulting number of possible routes, deriving predictions for other situations (for example, 'If there are 4 gaps and 3 gaps, there will be 12 different ways'.)

Floor robot

page 137

Using a programmable vehicle You may need to amend the assessment checklist on the sheet, as the functions available vary according to the model of floor robot used. Suitable vehicles for this task include PIXIE, Roamer and PIP. If the child is familiar with programmable vehicles, he/she may suggest ideas to try. Alternatively, present the child with a specific task such as:

• move in a square pathway (possibly one already marked on the floor);
• write over a giant letter or 'computer' numeral;
• send the vehicle away, turn it around and bring it back.

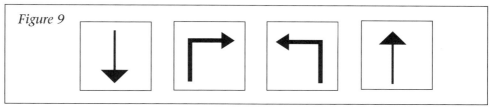

Figure 9

Some children will work on the task independently; others will need support. Function cards (see Figure 9) may help the child to sequence a set of movements before recording directly on the sheet. A young or inexperienced child may lack confidence in using a range of functions. Such a child may forget to clear the memory, and will use inappropriate key sequences that cause the robot to 'grumble'. At the next level of capability, a child will use forward/backward functions and may add pauses and sound (where available). The most able child will use angle (where available) to turn, and may begin to use the repeat facility (for example, when turning through four right angles to generate a square movement).

Hide and seek

page 138

Using co-ordinates to specify position This is a variation on the 'Battleships' game, and requires prior experience of working with co-ordinates. This sheet is particularly relevant to the content of the Scottish Guidelines for Mathematics 5–14. In preparing for the game, you will need to consider how children will shield their grids from one another. During the game, you will need to observe each child giving and receiving ordered pairs of co-ordinates to make sure that the x and y co-ordinates are being used in the conventional way (the x co-ordinate first).

Each player can use the lower section of the page to keep a running record of guesses he/she has made in trying to find her/his opponent's counters; this could be done by, for example, using counters for 'hits' and striking out 'misses' with a pencil. This chart also acts as a check at the end of the game, to make sure that there have been no errors or omissions. The child can make a permanent record of the game by drawing in the position of his/her counters, as well as detailing who he/she played and who won.

This is a relatively complex task, and the child may find the giving and receiving of instructions a challenge in itself. To some extent, the task will be differentiated by how well the child works without support; note the amount of support given to the child on the sheet. An able child will appreciate the need to address the horizontal co-ordinate first, and will accurately give and receive instructions.

Name

Date

Flat shapes

Demonstrates that the child can recognise, name, describe and draw 2D shapes.

Using and applying
• *Uses mathematical language to describe shapes.*

Cut the labels from the bottom of the page. Point to each shape and ask the child its name. Then ask the child to record by sticking down the labels, or by writing the names, in the spaces under the shapes. Now fold the sheet in half. Ask the child to draw one of each shape in the four empty boxes.

Note whether the child can name:
❑ triangle
❑ square
❑ rectangle
❑ circle

can draw:
❑ triangle
❑ square
❑ rectangle
❑ circle

Teacher comments:

Fold here.

Teachers' notes, page 109

✂ square | triangle | rectangle | circle

More 2D shapes

Name these shapes.

Demonstrates that the child can recognise, name and draw some less common 2D shapes.

Using and applying
• **Uses mathematical language to describe shapes.**

Cut the shape name labels off the bottom of the sheet. Give the child the labels one at a time to position and stick or copy into place on the top half of the sheet. Talk about the shapes, and scribe for the child if necessary. Then fold the sheet in half, so that the child cannot see the top half while drawing on the bottom half of the page.

Note whether the child can name and draw:
❑ name
❑ draw

❑ name
❑ draw

❑ name
❑ draw

Teacher comments:

Fold here.

Draw another oval, pentagon and hexagon in this space. Label them.

Teachers' notes, page 109

✂ -

| pentagon | oval | hexagon |

Name

Date

My first tangram

Demonstrates that the child can manipulate 2D shapes to make larger shapes or patterns. Demonstrates that the child can use mathematical language to describe shapes and patterns.

Using and applying
• *Explores possibilities.*

Provide the child with several 7cm × 7cm squares of paper or coloured card, a ruler, scissors and adhesive. Ask her/him to divide each square into four triangles (by drawing and cutting along diagonal lines), and then to combine the four triangles in a shape or pattern which he/she can stick down on the sheet. He/she should have several goes, continuing on the back of the sheet if necessary. Ask the child to describe her/his shapes.

Note whether the child:
❑ uses appropriate language
❑ recognises different orientations of the same shape
❑ names any regular shapes made

Teacher comments:

Teachers' notes, pages 109–110

Name

Date

Short straw, long straw

You need straws of two different lengths.

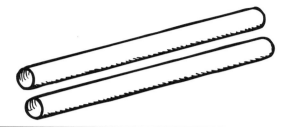

Demonstrates the child's ability to make and recognise triangles of different types.

Using and applying
• *Works systematically.*
• *Records work in pictorial form.*

Provide straws of two different lengths, ideally in two contrasting colours. Ask the child to make as many different triangles with these as possible. He/she should work with the straws on a large sheet of paper and record by drawing on the sheet, using coloured pencils. When he/she has finished, ask the child whether he/she thinks all the triangles have been found. What can he/she say about the properties of the different triangles?

Note whether the child:
❑ identifies similar and different triangles
❑ works methodically

Teacher comments:

How many different kinds of triangles can you make with these straws?

Have you found them all?

Teachers' notes, page 110

Name

Date

What's my rule?

Demonstrates the child's ability to sort shapes according to a rule (or identify a rule from a sort).

Using and applying
• *Selects the mathematics for the task.*
• *Talks about the work using geometrical language.*
• *Records in pictorial form.*

Provide a wide range of shapes (see Teachers' notes). Let the child handle and talk about a few of them. Now ask the child to put some of the shapes in the sorting ring, according to a 'secret' rule. After further discussion, ask the child to disclose the rule and to record it on the tag provided. Alternatively, place some shapes according to your own 'secret' rule and ask the child to guess it.

Note whether the child:
❑ recognises a rule
❑ invents and uses a rule

Shape words known/used:

Teacher comments:

My rule is

Name   *Date*

Is it half?

Demonstrates the child's ability to create and recognise half of a unit shape.

Using and applying
• *Finds ways of overcoming difficulties.*
• *Checks her/his work.*
• *Records work in diagrammatic form.*

Provide the child with a 16-pin geoboard or equivalent (if available) and some elastic bands. Explain that the task is to find different ways of dividing the board into two halves. Talk through the example shown. Let the child work on the geoboard (using elastic bands) and record solutions on the sheet. Encourage the child to check her/his work and talk about the strategies used.

Note whether the child:
❑ understands halves as two identical pieces
❑ understands halves as equal quantities
❑ checks her/his work
❑ talks about 'straight' and 'bent' (or 'broken') lines

Teacher comments:

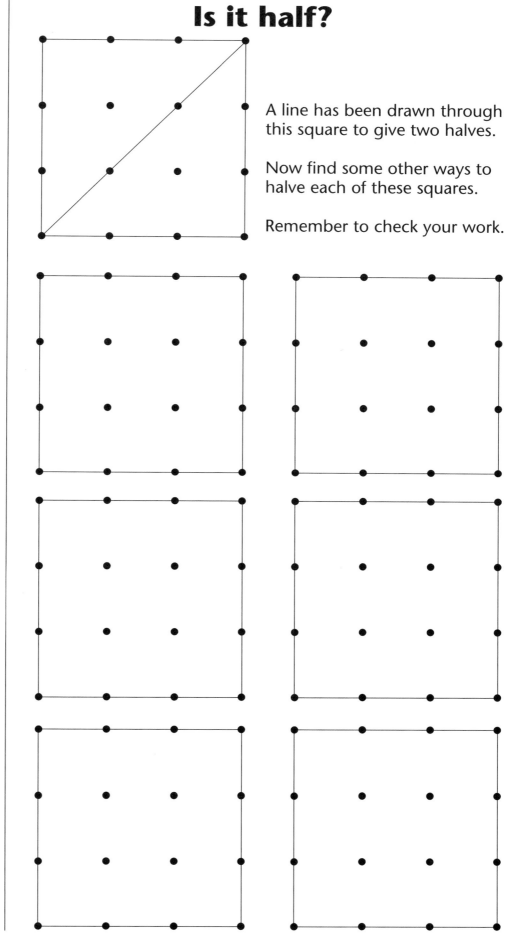

A line has been drawn through this square to give two halves.

Now find some other ways to halve each of these squares.

Remember to check your work.

Teachers' notes, pages 111–112

Name _____   *Date* _____

3D shape names

Demonstrates that the child can name and describe 3D shapes.

Using and applying
• *Uses appropriate mathematical language.*
• *Responds to a description.*
• *Gives a description.*

Give each child two of each of the six shapes listed. Point to each shape in turn and ask the child to name it. Record her/his success by ticking the appropriate boxes. Now ask the children to work in pairs (see Teachers' notes), describing shapes to each other and guessing each other's shapes. Record the child's descriptions of shapes in the speech bubbles.

Note whether the child can use the words:
❑ curved
❑ flat
❑ straight
❑ face
❑ edge
❑ side
❑ corner

Teacher comments:

I know the names of:

cone	sphere
cuboid	cylinder
cube	pyramid

What is the shape?

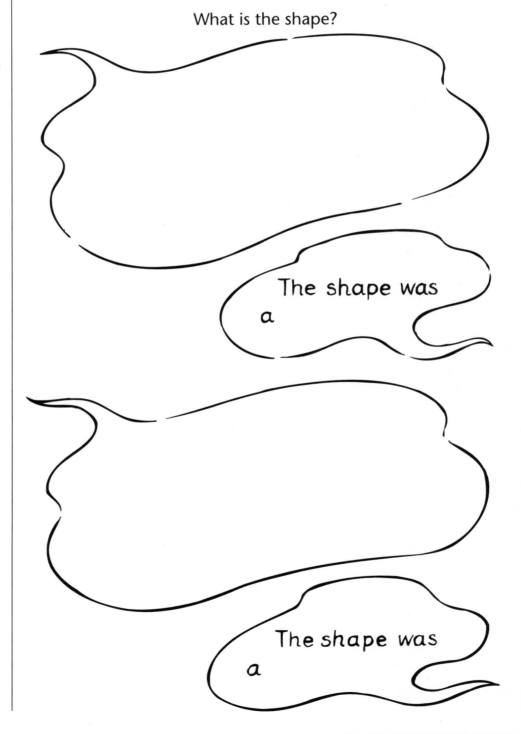

The shape was a

The shape was a

Teachers' notes, page 112

Name

Date

Does it roll? Does it build?

Using and applying
- *Predicts the outcomes.*
- *Checks her/his work.*
- *Presents findings.*

The child will need access to sets of cubes, cuboids, cones, spheres, cylinders and pyramids. Ask her/ him to predict the answers to the two questions, then to find the answers by rolling the shapes and building towers with them, and then to record her/his findings and describe them to you. Scribe for the child if necessary.

Note whether the child:
❑ uses appropriate vocabulary
❑ explains her/his findings
❑ makes generalisations

Teacher comments:

Does it roll?

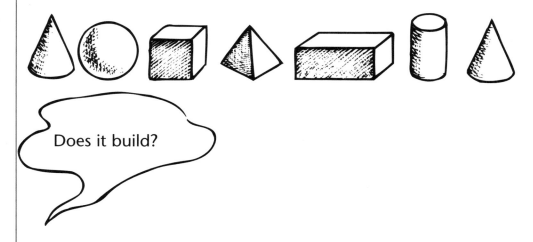

Does it build?

Teachers' notes, pages 112–113

Name   Date

Making boxes

Make a **cube**. Note the pieces you used.

Demonstrates that the child can construct 3D shapes from a construction kit. Demonstrates that the child can explore the 2D faces of a 3D shape.

Using and applying
• Uses equipment appropriately.
• Describes own work using mathematical language.
• Uses pictorial or written presentation.

Provide a construction kit which consists of flat tiles, such as Polydron or Clixi. Ask the child to work through the sheet, recording (by writing or drawing) the pieces he/ she has used to make each box.

Note whether the child:
❑ works methodically
❑ responds to the 3D shape names given
❑ records the flat faces used

Teacher comments:

Make a **triangular pyramid**. Note the pieces you used.

Make a **triangular prism**. Note the pieces you used.

Teachers' notes, page 113

Boxed in

This net can be folded to make an open box.

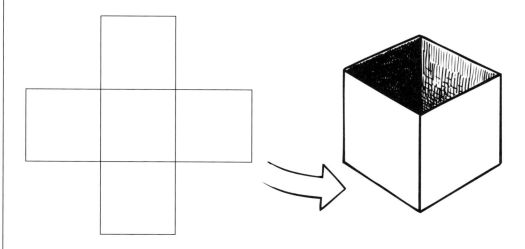

*Demonstrates the child's
ability to visualise and
make nets for a simple 3D
shape.*

Using and applying
• *Finds several options.*
• *Uses trial and
improvement.*
• *Records pictorially.*

Provide suitable
construction materials (if
available), or provide
sheets of card.
Demonstrate the example
at the top of the sheet,
then leave the child to
work on the task.
Encourage the child to
create the box shape and
then 'unpick' it in various
ways. Look at how the
child finds new nets.

Note whether the child:
❑ works independently
❑ works methodically

Teacher comments:

Find other nets that make a box just the same as the one above. Draw them here.

Have you found them all?

Name *Date*

Symmetrical or not?

Are these shapes symmetrical?
Draw in any lines of symmetry that you can find.

Demonstrates that the child can recognise a symmetrical shape and draw in a line of symmetry.

Using and applying
• *Uses equipment (mirror) appropriately.*
• *Checks work.*
• *Explains results.*

Give each child a small double-sided safety mirror, a ruler and a pencil. Read the question and instruction on the page to the child, then let her/him complete the task.

Note whether the child:
❑ recognises symmetrical shapes
❑ uses the mirror to check
❑ draws in a line of symmetry
❑ recognises shapes that have several lines of symmetry

Teacher comments:

Name

Date

Mirror image

I used these:

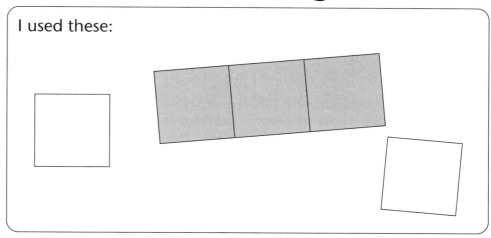

Demonstrates the child's ability to recognise and create shapes with reflective symmetry.

Using and applying
• *Uses strategies.*
• *Checks solutions.*
• *Talks about her/his work.*

Give each child five shapes corresponding to those shown (for example, card shapes or cubes) and a double-sided safety mirror. Explain what is meant by **reflective symmetry**, using the example provided. Demonstrate with the mirror if necessary. Now ask the child to make as many different symmetrical shapes as possible, using some or all of the pieces. The three-square section should not be broken up. The child should record each arrangement on the sheet, drawing in the lines of symmetry if he/she can.

Note whether the child:
❑ works without support
❑ checks her/his work (with the mirror)
❑ identifies reflective symmetry
❑ identifies rotational symmetry

Teacher comments:

I made these:

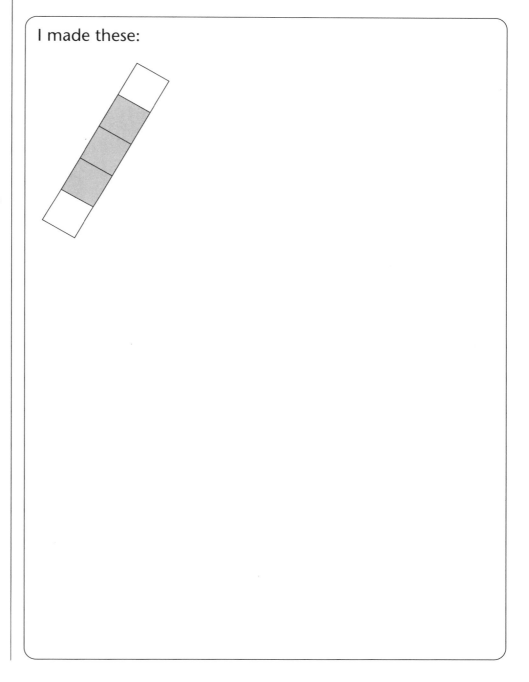

Teachers' notes, page 114

Name _____   *Date* _____

Fitting together

Tick the shapes that tessellate with each other.

My two shapes are: _____

_____

Here is my pattern:

Demonstrates that the child can determine which 2D shapes do or do not tessellate. Demonstrates that the child can tessellate using paired shapes.

Using and applying
• *Chooses own methods.*
• *Describes own work.*
• *Tries several patterns using two shapes.*

Give the child sets of the 2D shapes shown on the sheet. Ask the child to try to tessellate each shape, and then to tick those that do tessellate. Then ask the child to find any two regular shapes (not just those shown) that will make a tessellating pattern together, by drawing on the sheet.

Note whether the child:
❑ sorts the shapes correctly
❑ makes a more complex pattern
❑ explains findings

Teacher comments:

Teachers' notes, page 114

Name _____   *Date* _____

Looking around

Demonstrates that the child can recognise tessellation patterns.

Using and applying
• *Develops own method of recording.*
• *Discusses and describes own work.*

Give the child a copy of the sheet and a clipboard. Ask her/him to look around the classroom or school for patterns of tessellating shapes. (See Teachers' notes.) Ask the child to record four such patterns on the sheet.

Note whether the child:
❑ recognises tessellation in the environment
❑ conveys the nature of the tessellating pattern by recording

Teacher comments:

Teachers' notes, page 114

Name   *Date*

What comes next?

Demonstrates that the
child can recognise, copy
and continue repeating
patterns.

Using and applying
• *Devises own repeating
pattern.*
• *Makes predictions
related to simple patterns.*

Read the activity title to
the child. Ask the child to
look at each pattern and
describe it orally, then
continue it on the sheet.
Ask her/him to explain
how the pattern works.
Read the text at the top of
the right-hand column to
the child. Ask her/him to
devise and draw a pattern
in that column.

Note whether the child:
❑ continues a simple
pattern
❑ describes the pattern
❑ devises own pattern

Teacher comments:

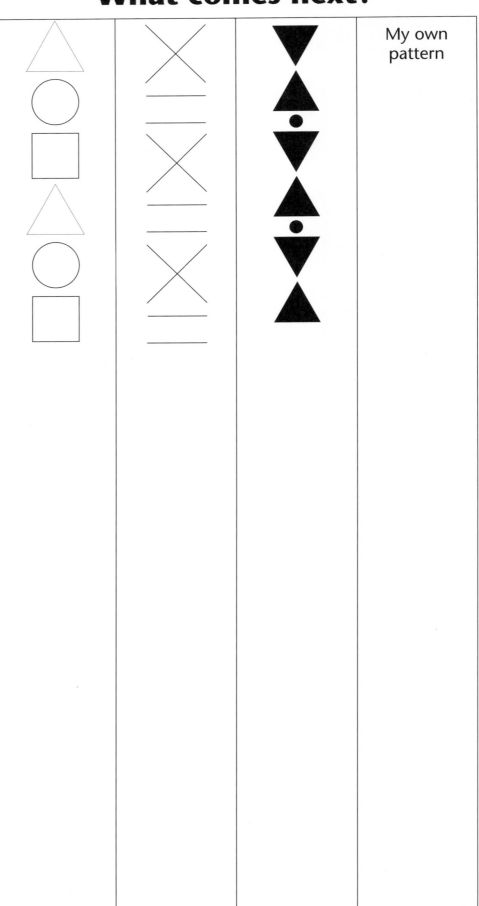

My own
pattern

Teachers' notes, page 115

132

Name _____ Date _____

Where are they?

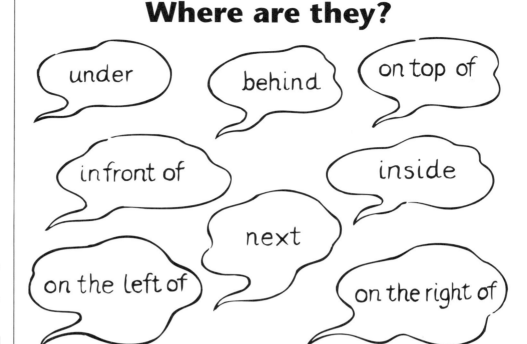

under

behind

on top of

in front of

inside

next

on the left of

on the right of

I can listen to these words and know where to go.

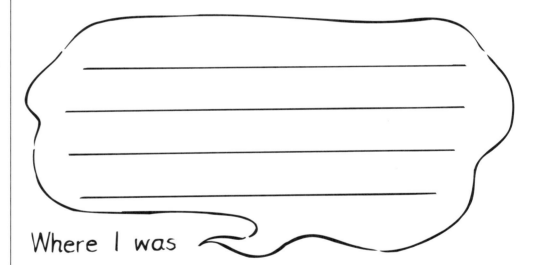

Where I was

Demonstrates that the child can understand, respond to and use positional language.

Using and applying
• **Uses maths in a classroom context.**

You will need a child's chair and some familiar objects for putting in different positions. Start with a group of children all facing the same way. Give individual children different positional instructions (see Teachers' notes). Then ask them to describe their positions to you. Use the sheet to record which instructions the child understands and responds to. Scribe the child's own description of her/his position on the sheet. Ask the child to draw a picture showing where he/she was.

Note whether the child:
❑ describes own position clearly, using correct language
❑ moves to correct position
❑ draws own position accurately

Teacher comments:

Teachers' notes, page 115

Name _____   *Date* _____

Spot the right angles

Demonstrates that the child can recognise a right angle in the context of the classroom.

Using and applying
• *Uses equipment for checking.*
• *Begins to make generalisations.*

Copy the sheet onto thin cards and cut off the bottom right-hand corner. Ask the child to personalise this with her/his name, then use it to find and/or check right angles on as many different objects and locations in the classroom as possible. Ask the child to record her/his findings on the sheet, encouraging generalisations.

Note whether the child:
❑ uses her/his right angle to check with
❑ recognises a right angle in most practical instances

Teacher comments:

Teachers' notes, page 115

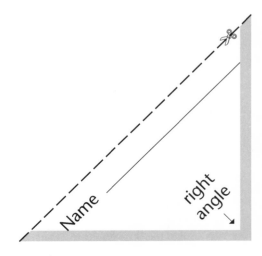

Name _____   Date _____

Turning

Demonstrates that the child can recognise how many times a tile has been turned. Demonstrates that the child can turn a tile through several $\frac{1}{4}$ turns and record the result.

Using and applying
• **Checks her/his own work.**
• **Makes predictions.**
• **Begins to generalise.**

Photocopy the sheet onto thin card. Cut off the picture tiles from the bottom of the sheet. In the first part of the task, ask the child to predict the outcome of each set of $\frac{1}{4}$ turn instructions and then to check using the tiles. In the second part of the task, ask the child to predict and draw the number of $\frac{1}{4}$ turns needed to get from each 'start' picture to the 'end' picture, then check using the tiles. The 'my check' boxes can be ticked to indicate correct predictions.

Note whether the child:
❏ predicts and records outcomes
❏ predicts and records turns
❏ checks predictions

Teacher comments:

Teachers' notes, page 116

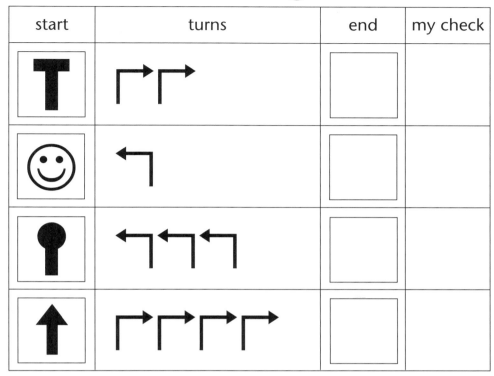

Name

Date

Gaps in the hedge

Demonstrates the child's ability to use networks. Demonstrates that the child can work systematically.

Using and applying
• *Works systematically.*
• *Finds some/all solutions.*
• *Predicts/generalises for similar tasks.*

You may prefer to make a 3D representation of this activity, using suitable obstructions and vehicles. Demonstrate the example provided and ask the child to find different ways through the gaps, recording them on the sheet. Observe to see how the task is managed. Then use the final question to encourage the child to predict, investigate and generalise.

Note whether the child:
❑ independently finds all the routes
❑ works systematically
❑ predicts for similar tasks

Teacher comments:

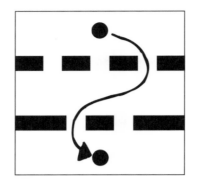

Here is a route to travel from one spot to another.

You may only pass through two gaps.

How many routes can you find, including the one above?

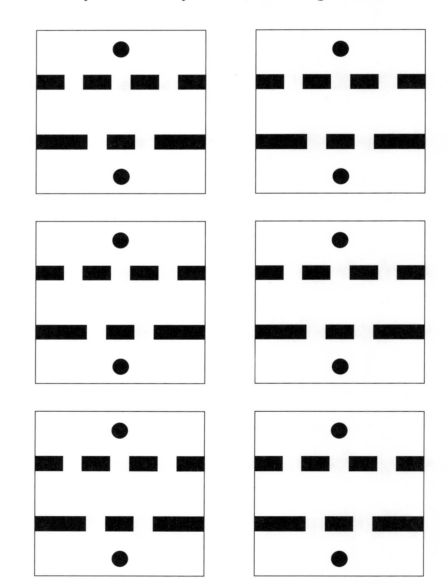

Have you found them all?
How many possible routes would there be if the lower hedge had three gaps in it? Or four gaps?

Floor robot

This is our robot:

I can make it follow this pathway:

I used these keys:

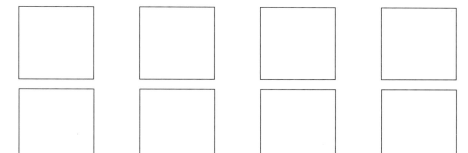

Teachers' notes, page 117

Name _____   Date _____

Hide and seek

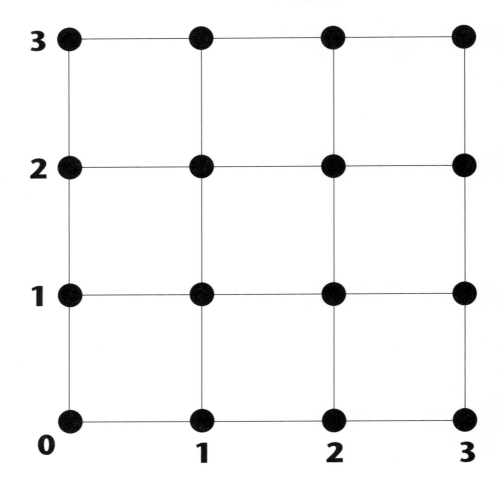

Demonstrates the child's ability to use co-ordinates to specify location.

Using and applying
• *Gives/follows instructions.*
• *Records graphically.*

This task is a game for two players. Each child needs a copy of the sheet and some small counters; the game also requires both players to conceal their boards. Each player places counters randomly on three of the grid spots. Players take turns to guess a pair of co-ordinates and record the other player's response (Yes or No) in some way on the chart of written co-ordinates. The winner is the first player to hit on all three of her/his opponent's counters. Finally, the child should record the outcome of the game at the bottom of the sheet.

Note whether the child:
❑ uses co-ordinates correctly
❑ takes turns
❑ gives instructions
❑ receives instructions
❑ works independently
❑ works with support
_____
_____
_____

Teacher comments:

(0,0)	(0,1)	(0,2)	(0,3)
(1,0)	(1,1)	(1,2)	(1,3)
(2,0)	(2,1)	(2,2)	(2,3)
(3,0)	(3,1)	(3,2)	(3,3)

I played with _____

I came

MEASURING

MEASURING

This chapter provides activities to assess children's capabilities in the following areas of measurement: length, area, mass, capacity and time. The activities cover:
- Early language of measurement and making comparisons.
- Measuring with non-standard units, leading to articulation of the need for standard units in measuring.
- Measuring with a variety of standard units linked to the scale of the items being measured.
- Measuring with a variety of equipment linked to the scale of the items being measured.

Prior knowledge and experience

As in other areas of mathematics, it is important to remember that a child may well have prior knowledge of some areas of measurement before starting Key Stage 1, depending on her/his experiences at home and in pre-school education. Some children will have weighed out ingredients in cooking, noticed distances on road signs, poured out water from bottles and containers in the bath or paddling pool, and both heard and talked about days of the week and times of the day in relation to their own activities. In school, children will continue to develop these skills and language through structured play, design and technology tasks and science, as well as maths.

Progression through Key Stage 1

In measurement, there are a number of skills and aspects of understanding to be acquired. The child may start by learning and using 'measuring' words such as *bigger*, *longer*, *wider*, *heavier* and *later* in her/his everyday experience. He/she child will need to refine these by applying them in the correct context, moving from general words such as *bigger* to specific mathematical terms such as *longer*, *wider* and *taller*.

UNITS OF MEASUREMENT

Using standard units

The child will begin to make comparisons and learn conservation in each area of measurement. When standard measures are introduced, some children may have heard or read words such as *metre*, *kilogram* and *litre*. The child may then need to learn how to match these units to the equipment used for measuring and to the type of measurement involved. When starting to discuss measurement children often suggest a measuring unit or piece of equipment but not necessarily the correct one.

Measurement and number skills

Children often start by making comparisons with a single large unit, such as 1 metre, 1 kilogram, 1 hour or 1 litre. When the child begins to work with smaller units such as cm, g, minutes or ml, there may be a mismatch between the child's measuring ability and her/his understanding of number (for example, ther child may be expected to measure up to 1m while still working on numbers to 10).) If the child works with half and quarter metres, or half hours, this should be linked to her/his understanding of how to find a half or a quarter of other things. If the child is working in units of 10cm (decimetres), this should be linked to her/his developing understanding of place value to 100 and to counting in steps of 10. If the child is working in units of 5 minutes, this can be linked to counting in fives or the five times table. In addition, the child's ability to count, read, write and order numbers to 100 and 1000 will also be important as he/she moves to using smaller units such as cm, g, minutes and ml.

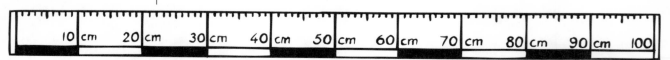

When the child moves on to comparison (for example, calculating how many cm longer something is, or how many more ml are needed) her/his understanding of number operations will be important. The child will need to understand how to find the difference between two amounts or lengths by counting on or back. If children find these numbers difficult to manipulate mentally, a calculator could be used.

MEASURING AND ESTIMATING

Measuring with accuracy

In developing measuring skills, it is important that the child becomes increasingly methodical and accurate in the use of equipment. Even when making initial comparisons of length, the child could be encouraged to place both objects so that their ends are together and look at the other end to see which is longer. Later, it is important that the child start with the ruler or tape measure at 0 or the measuring jug completely empty. When the teacher is assessing at each stage, it will be important to note the child's skills and methods in these areas as the expectation of accuracy increases.

Estimation, judgement and practical awareness

Alongside measuring with increasing accuracy, it is also important that the child learns how to estimate and builds up an ability to make sensible guesses. For example, the child could use a metre stick to develop a sense of whether something is more than, about or less than a metre. This will give the child a basis on which to make choices of equipment later – for example, choosing a ruler, a metre stick or a tape measure to measure the distance from one door to another along the school corridor.

ORGANISATION OF THE TASKS

All of these assessment tasks are structured in a similar way. The first part of the activity is a practical task or challenge for the child, working alone, with a partner or in a small group. The second part of the activity requires the child to work individually with an adult to record, explain and reflect upon the measuring task.

Key points for assessment

In the first part of the activity, the child might be observed to say or do something that it might be useful to note on her/his sheet, either to indicate her/his level of skill understanding to be clarified with the child later. In the second part of the activity, it is important to encourage the child to describe, explain and answer questions about her/his work, in order to learn more about the child's skills, knowledge and understanding. This is a valuable opportunity to help the child recognise what he/she has learned or improved upon, and to set future tasks. In all cases, the child's comments should be scribed if writing would make the task unduly laborious. After all, the key point of the tasks is to assess the child's skills and understanding in the area of measurement, not the child's writing proficiency.

USE OF EQUIPMENT

As the child becomes more competent in the different kind of measurement, he/she should be made aware of the potential choice of equipment. If the equipment to be used is always given directly to the child, he/she will not have any opportunity to demonstrate the knowledge that (for example) length is measured by certain pieces of equipment and not others. Within a given type of measurement, the child will also need to be able to choose the most appropriate piece of equipment (such as a ruler for a short, straight measurement of length). By encouraging the children to choose from a range of instruments rather than using a given piece, the teacher will be able to make a fuller assessment of some of the more challenging tasks.

TEACHING NOTES FOR INDIVIDUAL ACTIVITIES

Length

Longer and shorter

page 150

Comparing For this activity, you will need to collect a group of objects suitable for use in comparing and ordering lengths. The collection might include ribbons, string, wool, sticks, paintbrushes and pencils. Choose things that are easy to compare and do not have other distracting features.

In the first part of the task, encourage the child to use mathematical vocabulary. If the child uses only the most basic words such as 'big', 'small' or 'little', ask her/him if he/she can think of any other words to use. When the child is verbally comparing the two objects, listen again for appropriate use of mathematical language.

In the second part of the task, you may wish to help the child by providing a piece of wool (or string) the same length as the one drawn on the sheet. Observe how the child works. Some may cut at random and then compare, working by trial and error until they arrive at the two pieces they need, while others may compare lengths of wool directly before cutting. Either method is acceptable, but will be worth noting in the 'Teachers' comments' section on the sheet as an aspect of using and applying maths.

You may want to scribe any additional or alternative words used in this activity, especially if the child needs prompting to use the correct mathematical language. If so, it might mean that the child needs further experience in using this language in context. This task will also give you the opportunity to assess whether the child has understood the conservation of length when working with different objects.

Hands and feet

page 151

Non-standard measures In this activity, using cut-outs for units will help with consistent and accurate measuring techniques. It is a good idea to pair children with contrasting hand sizes together, to make the differences more obvious. The item to be measured should be large enough to measure with hands and feet, and be easily accessible so that the measuring does not interrupt other classroom activities. It could be a particular surface, a rug, a cupboard or a table-top. You may wish to draw or write this in the box on the sheet before photocopying it.

The final conclusions can be written by the child or scribed by an adult. The quality of these comments will be crucial in assessing the child's understanding of the need to use standard (as opposed to non-standard) measures of length. In addition, the child's method of measuring (carefully placing the unit end to end, or using it less precisely) and her/his use of mathematical language will be noteworthy. Some children will realise that the larger the handspan, the fewer such units will be needed to measure the object, and that different people's measurements are not comparable because the unit being used is not standard. You might ask questions such as 'In what other ways could you measure so you didn't have this problem?' to find out more about their thinking. If the child does not notice the difference in the measurements, or does not place any importance on it even when you draw her/his attention to it, it is clear that the child does not yet appreciate the need for standard measures.

Taller and shorter

page 152

Comparing to 1 metre It may be useful to have a set of name cards or a class list available for the child to use in writing names. If everyone in your class is taller than one metre, you might 'borrow' children from another class.

While the children are working, observe their Using and Applying skills:
• Does the child estimate first and then check?
• Does the child compare and record accurately?
• Does the child use mathematical language correctly?

A more able child may describe how much shorter or taller than 1m the children are. When the task is complete, ask each child to describe what he/she has found out. This will give you an opportunity to question further if you have missed an aspect of the work, or if the child has made a mistake.

You and me

page 153

Measuring in cm with a tape measure Try to pair the children so that the partners are not the same size, or the comparisons will be uninteresting. During the activity, you should be looking for the following:
• Does the child use the tape measure carefully, starting at one end of the body part and ending at the other end?
• Does the child read the length with the tape measure starting from 0, not from the start of the tape or from 1?
• Does the child adapt from measuring along to measuring around, according to what is being measured?

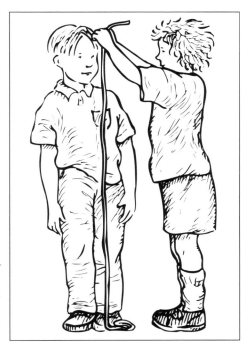

After the measuring is complete, the child should look at the results and draw some conclusions about what he/she has found out. Look for correct use of the words 'longer', 'longest', 'shorter', 'shortest' and 'the same as'. A more able child will tell you (or respond to questions about) how many cm more or less one length is relative to another, by finding the difference or counting on/back.

Estimating

page 154

Guessing and checking You will need to prepare the sheet by writing in a list of real things whose length can be estimated and measured by the child. For the cm section, you might use familiar classroom items such as pens, paintbrushes, glue spreaders, books or cassettes. For the m section, you might use the long side of a table, the sink, a bookshelf, a piece of carpet or the corridor. In these cases, you might mark where to start and end to make sure that the children are clear about what length is being looked at. You may prefer the children to attempt the cm section and return later to the m section, in which case the date should be added to each section.

The child should be able to make a sensible guess which is not wildly inaccurate. The child's guesses may improve during the activity, as her/his measuring experience is related back to the estimating task. After the activity, talk to the child to find out what he/she noticed about the relationship between guesses and measurements. A more able child might state in numerical terms how different her/his guesses and measurements were. If you had to help the child to measure accurately, note this fact.

Measuring in metres
page 155

Longer lengths Select appropriate distances for the child to measure. Include some distances which involve going round a corner. You may wish to choose distances which require the children to decide to round up or down to the nearest metre or half metre. You should keep a note on a master sheet

of the correct measurement for each distance, so the child can be asked to check again if her/his measurement is wrong. It is a good idea to mark the start and end of each distance, so that there are no misunderstandings.

During the task you might look out for the way that the child uses the measuring instrument, as well as how he/she solves difficulties such as going round corners and recording a result that is not exactly a metre. Children with well-developed measuring skills may record using cm for parts of metres, or may round up or down. Some children might refer to half or quarter metres if they are familiar with these terms from other work. In their final comments, children should show awareness that a metre string is the best instrument for measuring length around a corner.

Area
Covering up
page 156

Non-standard measures Choose a suitable flat surface to be covered, such as a rug, table top or large carrier bag. Make sure it is easily accessible and not being used by others, so that the measuring does not interrupt other classroom tasks. The collection of 'units' to measure with should include some that will not cover the area, such as coins or irregular shapes.

When you are discussing the child's results with her/him, you might ask the following questions:
• Why does it take more of some units than others to cover the area? This might help to indicate the child's understanding of the problems of using non-standard measures.
• What sort of unit was best for covering? This might show whether the child has thought about how what was provided affected the task. For example, the child might realise that using postage stamps to measure a very large area is an inappropriate choice because of the numbers and time required; or that using coins would not be appropriate because they would not cover the area.

• What did you do about small areas that were left uncovered because of the size of unit? The child might have disregarded these, or grouped them together and estimated.

• How were the units chosen? – for example, why circular tiles or coins were not used.

Mass

Heavier and lighter

page 157

Comparing For this activity, you will need to collect three items for each child with a difference in mass between them that the child can recognise by holding and handling. In comparing them, it is important that the child uses the words 'heaviest' and 'lightest' and no words related to other attributes such as the size, colour, shape or material. In the second part of the activity, listen for correct use of the words 'heavier' and 'lighter'. In the third part of the activity, bring a small group of children together around the table. Allow the children to experiment with the items until they have found the ones they want. Observe how each child tries to find a heavier and a lighter thing. You may wish to scribe all of the vocabulary the child uses, especially if the child needs prompting to use mathematical terms.

Balancing

page 158

Non-standard measures A suitable object to measure might be an apple, a ball, a cup, a book, a shoe or a lump of Plasticine. While the child is balancing the object, look to observe whether he/she works methodically, counting the smaller objects into the pan, or just concentrates on balancing and then counts afterward. You should also note whether he/she uses the balance correctly. The child's suggestions about why it took different numbers of the different units to balance the item will give you an opportunity to find out whether he/she understands the need for standard measures. Some children will be able to explain why it took less of some units and more of others to balance the same object; others will accept the fact without employing the mathematical concept of mass.

My mass

page 159

Using kg and bathroom scales When working in the group, each child should have the opportunity to make a full set of measurements. The child might need help to round masses up or down to the nearest kg. When the child is working individually, listen for the use of mathematically correct language in making comparisons. A more able child might be expected to refine the comparisons by saying how many more kg one child weighs than another. It might be a good idea to avoid possible distress by grouping together children of similar mass.

MEASURING

A kilogram

page 160

Making up to a kg Observe the child working. He/she will have the opportunity to estimate, check and retry. You should note the child's methods, especially if he/she devises a way of working methodically. A more able child should realise that it is pointless to combine all the heavier items, as together they will be too heavy. In the child's comments, look for awareness that a small number of heavier objects weighs the same as a larger number of lighter objects.

Measuring with grams

page 161

Using kitchen scales Keep a note of the mass of each object you have provided for the assessment, to use when checking the child's work. During the task, look for correct use of the scales and accurate reading of the dial.

After the task, you might ask questions to see whether the child can tell you how many more grams one item is than another. This will be more appropriate for a child who is confident about using mental methods to add and take away numbers to 100 and beyond. If you feel that a child knows what to do but cannot work with such large numbers, suggest that he/she uses a calculator.

Capacity

If the children are working with water, you may wish to scribe their results for them in order to prevent sheets from getting wet and disintegrating.

Which holds more?

page 162

Comparing There should be a range of containers available, so that the child can compare some containers that are similar in capacity but different in size and shape. You may wish to provide funnels for pouring, if some of the containers have narrow openings. While the children are working, observe the method each child uses and how careful he/she is in pouring. The child might choose to fill the smaller container and pour it into the larger, or vice versa. Either method is viable; what matters is the child's understanding of the meaning of the result.

A more able child might be able to comment on the results by telling you that one container held a lot more than another, whereas another pair were nearly the same. Throughout, you should be noting the child's language and whether he/she uses the words 'most/least' and 'hold more/holds less' appropriately. Look for evidence of success or improvement in predicting relative capacity.

Fill the pot

page 163

Non-standard measures The large container or 'pot' could be (for example) a vase, a tub or a saucepan. The capacity units given on the chart can be replaced with others if necessary. Keep a note of how many of each unit is needed, as a reference for checking the child's results. The child should work through the sheet first guessing, then measuring. While the child works, you should note her/his accuracy in pouring, counting and recording.

After the child has finished, discuss her/his estimating skills. Were the guesses sensible? Did they improve with time? The child might refine her/his estimating skills quickly as he/she works, reacting to the measurement that he/she does. You should question the child to find out whether he/she understands that fewer of a bigger unit will be needed to fill the pot, and more of a smaller unit.

MEASURING

More or less than 1 litre

page 164

Making up to 1 litre Provide the group with a collection of (at least) ten containers, five of which hold less and five of which hold more than a litre, including some that are close to a litre either way. Observe the child's use of the measuring jug to see whether he/she uses the units marked correctly and carefully. You should also observe the child's method. Some children may fill the container and then pour the contents into the measuring jug; others may measure a litre and pour this into the chosen container. Either method is valid. In the child's description, listen for correct and clear use of the mathematical language of comparison. A more able child might be able to tell you how much more/less than a litre a container measured by reading the scale or estimating beyond it.

Measuring with ml

page 165

For this task, you should provide a range of measuring jugs (500ml, 1 litre, 2 litres) as well as at least three containers in each range. Keep a note of the actual capacity of each container (in ml or l) to help in checking the children's work. During the task, you should observe whether the child uses the measuring jugs correctly and reads the scales accurately. After the task, a more able child might be able to tell you the difference in ml between two containers. If a child knows what to do but cannot manipulate numbers of that size mentally, you might suggest that he/she uses a calculator.

Time

Before and after

page 166

Ordering events The focus of this task is on using the words *before* and *after*. In the second part of the task, the order of the two events is not as important as the understanding of the word 'before' and the ability to think of things just before an event, rather than during the day. For the third part of the task, select three events related to classroom routine that happen in a known order and are familiar to the children – for example, eating their snack, putting their coats on, going out to play. The child should order these events using their experience, and describe them using appropriate vocabulary listed on the sheet. If the child does not use the expected vocabulary, question her/him and note her/his understanding of these words when they are used by someone else.

What can we do in one minute?

page 167

Using a minute timer, making comparisons You will need to prepare this activity with the appropriate materials: four 1-minute timers; beads and shoelaces; Unifix or Multifix cubes; paper and pencils; a sheet with circles drawn on and scissors.

The child's comments on the pair's results should be noted at the bottom of the sheet. You might prompt appropriate comments by asking questions such as the following:
- Who could thread the most beads?
- Who was faster at writing her name? Why?
- Who was slower at sticking cubes together?
- Which was the slowest thing to do? Why?
- What would happen if you had two minutes?

With more able children, you might ask:
- How many more beads did _____ thread than _____?
- How many fewer circles did _____ cut out than _____?

Running races
page 168

Timing in seconds, comparing times Work in athletics could provide a context for this activity. The children in the group should each run alone, to give the others opportunities to time with the stopwatch. The ordering task will indicate whether the child understands that the smallest number of seconds means the fastest runner, and vice versa. The child should describe the results using the terms fastest/slowest, and possibly using ordinal numbers. A more able child might compare times by calculating many more/less seconds one child took than another. Watch out for confusion between time and speed – for example, '3 seconds faster' is incorrect but '3 seconds less, so faster' would be correct.

How long are the holidays?
page 169

Using a calendar Offer a variety of familiar calendars, or provide photocopies of appropriate pages if you think it will be useful for the children to mark on the calendars. Select an appropriate school holiday; this could be one relevant to the timing of the activity in the school year, or could be chosen to match the children's numerical skills.

Look for the accurate use of the calendar to find the information required. You should also note the child's strategies. Some children might find the first date on the calendar and simply count the days until they reach the end date. Other children might use the calendar to check the number of days in the month (where relevant) and then use their number skills to calculate the number of days in the holiday. This task gives you an opportunity to assess the child's ability to work in an organised, methodical way. The child's response to the final question is an important indicator of this; you might prompt the child to justify her/his methods in this section.

MEASURING

Telling the time: o'clock and half past The completed sheet should be analysed to see whether any errors are related to careless recording or to incomplete understanding of how to read and record on the analogue and/or digital clock. The child should be given the opportunity to talk about her/his recording, to help you assess whether it is the child's understanding or her/his recording that needs more work.

Likely errors are as follows:
Analogue
O'clock – both hands are long, though in the correct positions.
Half past – both hands are long, though in the correct positions.
Half past – the short hand is not in between the numerals.
Digital
Half past – the digits are not placed correctly, for example 40:30 instead of 04:30.

Telling the time: quarter to/past and other time intervals This assessment could be used immediately after the previous one; or there could be a gap to allow for the further learning that is called for. The child should be allowed to choose her/his own methods for working out the duration of each event. Note any revealing comments or actions. For example, children may apply their knowledge of the five times table when counting in minutes or a child might count on or back. Asking the child to make up her/his own example could give you the opportunity to extend a child who has worked out the times accurately by trying some more difficult start and end times.

Matching equipment and units to appropriate type of measurement This activity will give you the opportunity to find out more about the child's awareness of different types of measurement, measuring equipment and units of measurement. You can structure the task (by your choice of questions) so that the child is sorting and recording one of each type of instrument, or have several examples of each type. Instruments used might include:
- Length – tape measure, ruler, metre stick.
- Mass – bathroom scales, kitchen scales, balance.
- Capacity – jug, bottle, spoon.
- Time – analogue clock, digital clock, stopwatch, calendar, diary.

Ask the child what could be measured, to allow her/him to suggest a range of real-life measuring experiences. Alternatively, prepare a set of challenges that the child can respond to practically, with either you or the child recording the outcomes. The following are possible examples:
- **Length**
'How tall is your teddy?'
'How long is your teddy's arm?'
'How much taller are you than your teddy?'
- **Mass**
'How much does your teddy weigh?'
'How much more do you weigh than your teddy?'
- **Capacity**
'How much water does it take to fill your teddy's bath?'
- **Time**
'How old is your teddy?'
'When is your teddy's birthday?'
'How long does it take to tie a bow around your teddy's neck?'

Longer and shorter

Demonstrates that the child can use specific mathematical vocabulary related to length. Demonstrates that the child can make comparisons and order objects based on length.

Using and applying
• *Selects maths for the task.*
• *Represents using pictures and objects.*
• *Talks about the work.*

Provide a collection of suitable objects (see 'Teachers' notes'). Let the child select three objects to work with. Ask her/him to find the longest and shortest of these, recording pictorially on the sheet. Now ask the child to compare two items verbally. Give her/him some wool and a pair of safety scissors. Ask the child to cut one piece of wool (or string) longer and one shorter than the one on the sheet, and stick them in place.

Note whether the child:
uses vocabulary correctly
❏ longest
❏ shortest
❏ is longer than
❏ is shorter than

uses suitable methods
❏ compares
❏ orders

Teacher comments:

is the longest.

is the shortest.

is longer than

is shorter than

longer

shorter

Teachers' notes, page 142

Name   *Date*

Hands and feet

Demonstrates that the child can measure length using non-standard units. Demonstrates that the child understands and can explain the need for a standard unit to measure with.

Using and applying
• *Selects maths for the task.*
• *Talks about her/his work.*
• *Responds to 'What would happen if...?' questions.*

Before the task, each child needs to draw around and cut out two of her/his hand shapes and foot shapes. The children will need to work in pairs for this activity, with one sheet per child. Choose the pairs carefully to ensure difference in results. Each pair should choose something to measure (see 'Teachers' notes') with their cut-out hands and feet, recording the item and their measurements on both sheets. Discuss their findings individually, scribing conclusions for the child if necessary. Include a question about what would happen if the child used a bigger/ smaller hand or foot.

Note whether the child:
❑ uses non-standard measurement units correctly
❑ explains why the measurements are different

Teacher comments:

We measured the length of

It took ☐ of <u>my</u> hand.

It took ☐ of _____ hand.

It took ☐ of <u>my</u> foot.

It took ☐ of _____ foot.

Why are the measurements different for different people?

_____

_____

_____

Why might this be a problem?

_____

_____

_____

Name *Date*

Taller and shorter

Im →

Demonstrates that the child can use a metre stick as a standard measure. Demonstrates that the child can use specific mathematical vocabulary related to height.

Using and applying
• **Uses maths equipment.**
• **Talks about the work.**
• **Records results in written or pictorial form.**

Tape a metre stick to the wall or door frame. Ask the child to measure her/ his friends' height against it and record in the chart whether they are taller or shorter than 1m (by writing names in the appropriate columns).

Note whether the child:
❑ uses the metre stick correctly
❑ records measurements in the correct columns
❑ responds to and uses the word 'taller'
❑ responds to and uses the word 'shorter'

Teacher comments:

taller than 1m	shorter than 1m

Teachers' notes, page 143

Name

Date

You and me

Demonstrates that the child can use a tape measure to measure with, reading centimetre measurements from a scale and making comparisons based on the results.

Using and applying
- **Uses appropriate equipment accurately.**
- **Explains results.**

Each child should work with a partner to take the body measurements and record them on her/his individual sheet. Encourage each child to comment individually on the results and what they indicate, either by writing or by dictating to you.

Note whether the child:
❑ uses a tape measure correctly
❑ records in cm
❑ makes verbal comparisons (longer/shorter)
❑ records how many cm (longer/shorter)

Teacher comments:

Body part	My friend	me
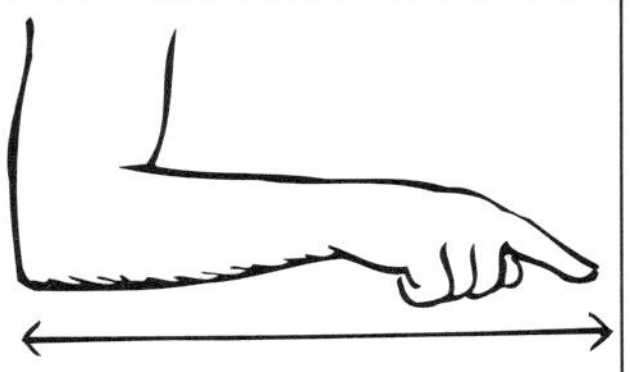 elbow fingertip		
 around the head		
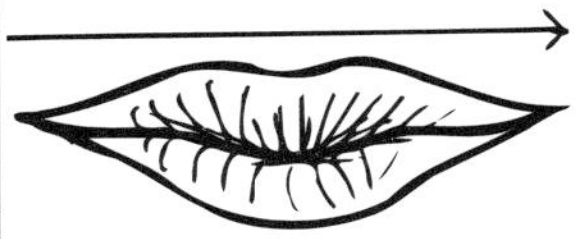 length of lips		
 across the shoulders		
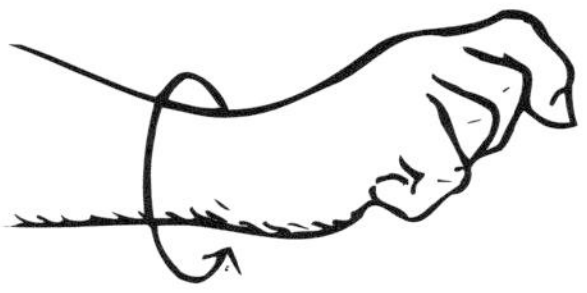 around the wrist		

What I found out:

_____

_____

_____

_____

_____

Teachers' notes, page 143

Name   *Date*

Estimating

Measure in cm	Estimate	Measurement
	_____ cm	_____ cm

_____

_____

_____

Measure in m	Estimate	Measurement
	_____ m	_____ m

_____

_____

Demonstrates that the child can estimate sensibly using cm and m.

Using and applying
- *Checks own results.*
- *Talks about the work.*

Before copying the sheet, fill in the boxes at the left-hand side of each chart with the names or pictures of real-life objects to be measured. (See Teachers' notes.) Ask the child to estimate the length of each object in the unit required, record the estimate and then check it by measuring with accuracy (using a tape measure). Finally, ask the child to compare the estimates with the measurements; comments can be recorded (by you or the child) underneath each chart.

Note whether the child:
makes a sensible estimate
❑ cm
❑ m

measures accurately to check
❑ cm
❑ m

❑ comments appropriately on the two results

Teacher comments:

Teachers' notes, pages 143–144

SCHOLASTIC PORTFOLIO ASSESSMENT
Maths Key Stage 1

Name   *Date*

Measuring in metres

from _____	to _____	Measurement	I used
			1m tape 1m stick 1m string
			1m tape 1m stick 1m string
			1m tape 1m stick 1m string
			1m tape 1m stick 1m string
			1m tape 1m stick 1m string
			1m tape 1m stick 1m string

Comments:

_____

_____

_____

_____

Demonstrates that the child can measure accurately in metres, using a metre stick, string or tape, and record the results.

Using and applying
• *Chooses appropriate measuring instrument.*
• *Solves problems.*

Prepare the sheet (before copying) by filling in the locations of distances to be measured (see 'Teachers' notes'). Provide the children with metre strings, 1m tape measures and metre sticks. After the task, ask each child why he/she used particular instruments in given cases; comments can be recorded (by you or the child) at the bottom of the sheet.

Note whether the child:
❑ measures accurately in metres
❑ chooses appropriate instrument and justifies his/her choice

records in between measurements by
❑ rounding up to the nearest metre
❑ rounding down to the nearest metre
❑ rounding up/down to the nearest $\frac{1}{2}$ metre
❑ measuring in cm

Teacher comments:

Teachers' notes, page 144

Covering up

Demonstrates that the child can use non-standard units to measure an area.

Using and applying
• *Uses experience of 2D shape to justify choice of unit.*
• *Devises own methods to deal with uncovered parts of the area.*

Provide a suitable surface and a collection of different shapes to use as measurement units (see Teachers' notes). Ask the child to choose three different units to measure the area of the same surface, then record the results on the sheet. Ask the child (and observe) what he/she did about space left over. Ask the child about the units used and scribe comments about their shape and size and the number required.

Note whether the child:
❑ places units carefully (edge to edge)
❑ explains choice of units
❑ explains why more of some units were needed than others

Teacher comments:

I was covering the

I used _____ to cover with.

It took _____ of these units.

I used _____ to cover with.

It took _____ of these units.

I used _____ to cover with.

It took _____ of these units.

Comments:

Teachers' notes, pages 144–145

Heavier and lighter

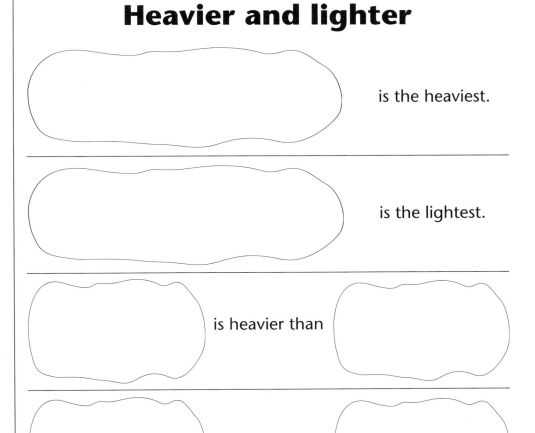

is the heaviest.

is the lightest.

is heavier than

is lighter than

Demonstrates that the child can use specific mathematical vocabulary related to mass. Demonstrates that the child can order objects and make comparisons based on mass.

Using and applying
• *Selects maths for the task.*
• *Represents using pictures or objects.*
• *Talks about the work.*

This is a small-group activity. Give each child three objects of different masses. Ask her/him to handle them and tell you which is heaviest and lightest, then record on the sheet (using pictures). Then ask the child to compare two of the three items, describe the difference in their mass and record pictorially on the sheet. Finally, pool all the objects used by the group. Give each child one item and ask her/him to draw it, and then to find and draw one item that is heavier and one that is lighter.

Note whether the child:
uses vocabulary correctly
❑ heaviest
❑ lightest
❑ is heavier than
❑ is lighter than

uses appropriate methods
❑ compares correctly
❑ orders correctly

Teacher comments:

heavier

lighter

Teachers' notes, page 145

Name   *Date*

Balancing

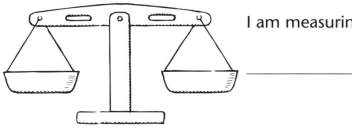

I am measuring the mass of

_____

Demonstrates that the child can measure mass using non-standard units with pan balance.

Using and applying
• *Selects maths for the task.*
• *Responds to 'What would happen if...' questions.*
• *Talks about the work.*

Give the child a pan balance and an object (see Teachers' notes) to be measured against a number of different units of mass (such as marbles, cubes, screws and cotton reels). Ask her/him to balance the object three times, using a different unit each time. The child should record the units used and the results on the sheet. Finally, ask the child to explain why it took different numbers of each unit to balance the chosen object, and to say what would happen if he/she used a different unit. You may need to scribe her/his responses.

Note whether the child:
❑ uses a pan balance correctly
❑ uses non-standard units accurately
❑ explains why the results are different

Teacher comments:

I used _____

_____ have the same mass as _____

I used _____

_____ have the same mass as _____

I used _____

_____ have the same mass as _____

What I found out:

_____

_____

_____

_____

Teachers' notes, page 145

SCHOLASTIC PORTFOLIO ASSESSMENT
Maths Key Stage 1

Name Date

My mass

Me ______ kg	______ ______ kg	______ ______ kg	______ ______ kg

Our masses in order

H L

Comments

______

______

______

______

______

______

Demonstrates that the child can use bathroom scales to measure in kg, reading kg from the dial. Demonstrates that the child can make comparisons based on measurements of mass.

Using and applying

- ***Uses appropriate equipment accurately.***
- ***Explains results.***

Provide each group of four children with a set of bathroom scales. Give each child a copy of the sheet. Ask each child to measure his/her mass and that of the other three children, using the scales. Then ask the child to reorder the results from the heaviest to the lightest, working independently, and to comment on the results. Scribe the child's comments if necessary.

Note whether the child:

❑ reads from the dial correctly
❑ orders from heaviest to lightest
❑ makes comparisons (heavier/lighter)
❑ makes numerical comparisons (kg lighter/ heavier)

Teacher comments:

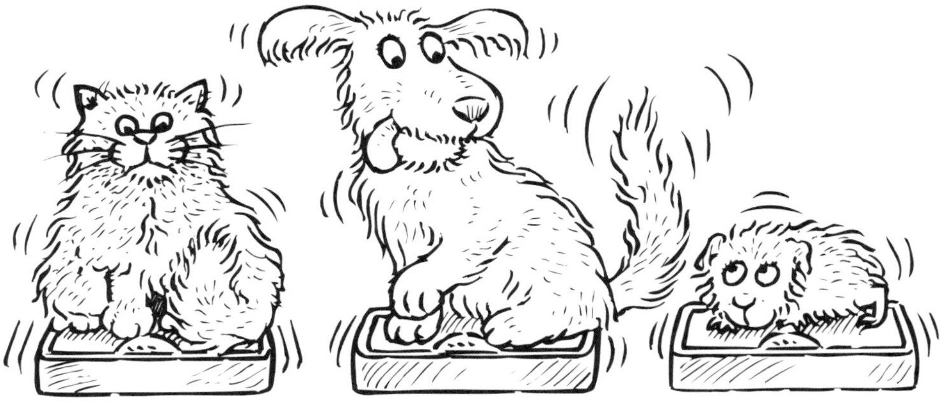

Teachers' notes, page 145

A kilogram

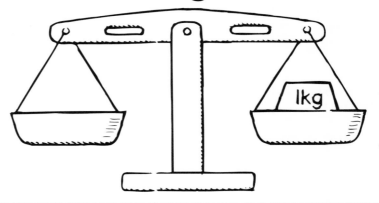

Demonstrates that the child can balance objects against a standard unit (1kg) using a pan balance appropriately.

Using and applying
- *Makes predictions.*
- *Checks predictions.*
- *Uses trial and improvement.*
- *Describes own work.*

Provide the child with a 1kg mass and access to a collection of lighter objects. Encourage the child to find combinations of objects that have about the same mass as 1kg. The child should use the balance to check, then record successful combinations on the sheet. Ask the child to comment on what he/she has found out; scribe the response if necessary.

Note whether the child:
❏ groups objects sensibly
❏ uses the balance appropriately

Teacher comments:

These objects have about the same mass as 1kg:	
	1kg
	1kg
	1kg

Comments:

Teachers' notes, page 146

Name

Date

Measuring with grams

Demonstrates that the child can read and compare measurements in g from a kitchen scales dial.

Using and applying
• Uses measuring equipment accurately.

Provide the child with a kitchen scales and a collection of everyday items suitable for the task. Ask the child to choose items from the group and measure their mass with the kitchen scales, in order to find three items to write into each section on the sheet. Alongside the name of each item, the child should record its mass in g. Encourage the child to identify the heaviest and lightest item in each group of three, ticking the appropriate box in each case.

Note whether the child can:
❏ measure in grams using dial of kitchen scales
❏ sort the measurements into the correct ranges
❏ find the heaviest/ lightest item in each group

Teacher comments:

less than 250g

Item	Mass (g)

heaviest in this group

between 250g and 500g

Item	Mass (g)

lightest in this group

between 500g and 1kg

Item	Mass (g)

heaviest in this group

Teachers' notes, page 146

Name _____ *Date* _____

Which holds more?

Demonstrates that the child can compare two containers to find which holds more.

Using and applying
* ***Devises a method to make the comparison.***
* ***Describes what he/she did.***

Provide a group of children with a variety of (numbered) containers. Ask the child to choose two and find out which holds more water (or dry sand). He/she should record the numbers and a picture on the sheet, and go on to investigate two more pairs of containers. Finally, ask the child to comment on the results; scribe her/his response if necessary, and encourage the child to draw a picture.

Note whether the child uses the terms:
❑ holds more than
❑ holds less than

Teacher comments:

I used

☐ and ☐

☐ held more

☐ held less

I used

☐ and ☐

☐ held more

I used

☐ and ☐

☐ held more

How I found out:

Teachers' notes, page 146

Fill the pot

Demonstrates that the child can measure capacity using non-standard units. Demonstrates that the child can estimate sensibly.

Using and applying
• *Records using a chart.*
• *Talks about the work.*

The child will need a large container to measure and various smaller containers (as indicated on the sheet) to use as capacity units. Encourage the child to guess how many units will be needed to fill the container each time, before measuring with dry sand or water. Talk about the results and ask the child to comment on her/his findings. You may wish to scribe the child's guesses, results and comments.

Note whether the child:
❑ works carefully
❑ records on the chart accurately
❑ makes sensible estimates
❑ explains findings in terms of the size of containers

Teacher comments:

I am filling

I used	My guess	My result
a paint pot		
an eggcup		
a teacup		
a spoon		

Comments

_____

_____

_____

_____

_____

_____

Teachers' notes, page 146

Name

Date

More or less than 1 litre

Demonstrates that the child can use a standard unit (1l) to compare with, using a measuring jug to find whether other containers have a capacity above or below 1 litre.

Using and applying
• *Uses a measuring jug appropriately.*
• *Makes predictions.*
• *Checks predictions.*
• *Describes the work.*

Provide the child with a 1 litre measuring jug and access to water or dry sand. The group will also need a selection of other containers (see 'Teachers' notes'). Ask the child to find and record five containers that hold less than 1l and five that hold more than 1l. After the child has completed the chart, ask her/him what method he/she used. Scribe the child's response if necessary.

Note whether the child:
❑ works accurately to measure out 1 litre each time
❑ pours carefully
❑ records results accurately

Teacher comments:

more than 1 litre	less than 1 litre

Comments:

Teachers' notes, page 147

Measuring with ml

Demonstrates that the child can read measurements (ml) from a scale and record them in ml or l in a given range.

Using and applying
- *Makes predictions.*
- *Checks predictions.*

Provide the child with a collection of numbered containers that cover the range indicated on the sheet, and a range of measuring jugs. The child should choose some containers and use the measuring jugs to find their capacity and record three in each section of the sheet (naming the item and giving its capacity). Encourage the child to identify the containers which contain most and least in each group of three.

Note whether the child:
❑ measures accurately in ml
❑ sorts measurements into the correct range
❑ finds the highest and lowest values in each group

Teacher comments:

less than 500ml

Item	ml

tick which holds most

between 500ml and 1 litre

Item	ml

tick which holds least

more than 1 litre

Item	l/ml

tick which holds least

Teachers' notes, page 147

Name

Date

Before and after

Demonstrates that the child can use specific mathematical vocabulary related to time.
Demonstrates that the child can order events.

Using and applying
• *Selects maths for the task.*
• *Talks about the work.*

Ask the child to draw something he/she does in the morning before lunchtime and something he/she does in the afternoon, after lunchtime. Scribe a descriptive sentence under each picture for the child. Then ask the child to draw two things he/she does before going to bed. Then offer three events from familiar classroom routine for the child to order and describe using time words (see below).

Note whether the child uses and responds to vocabulary:

uses   responds
❑   ❑ before
❑   ❑ after
❑   ❑ next
❑   ❑ sooner
❑   ❑ later

Teacher comments:

At lunchtime I

eat my lunch.

In the evening

I go to bed.

Teachers' notes, page 147

Name   Date

What can we do in one minute?

Demonstrates that the child can use a timer to measure one minute and make comparisons of speed.

Using and applying
- *Makes comparisons.*
- *Explains results.*

Each child should work with a partner, but record both their results on her/his own sheet. Set up the four tasks, with a minute timer at each. The children should time each other, allowing 1 minute for each task, then record how much was done. Ask each child to describe and explain the results individually. Scribe the child's response.

Note whether the child:
❑ uses the timer appropriately
❑ describes the results

uses vocabulary
❑ faster/slower
❑ more/less

Teacher comments:

What we did	me	my friend
thread beads		
stick cubes together		
write name		
cut out circles		

Teachers' notes, pages 147–148

Name   *Date*

Running races

Demonstrates that the child can use a stopwatch to measure time in seconds.
Demonstrates that the child understands times as relative inverse measures of speed.

Using and applying
- ***Uses equipment accurately and appropriately.***
- ***Describes results.***
- ***Interprets results.***

Mark out a suitable distance to run (back and forth or around). Divide the children into groups of four. Give each group a stopwatch to time the running. They should run one at a time. Each child should record all the group's results. Encourage the children to work independently on the sheet, ordering and describing the results.

Note whether the child:
❑ uses a stopwatch appropriately
❑ records results
❑ describes using terms fastest/slowest
❑ compares times in seconds (eg '3 seconds longer')

Teacher comments:

Me	_____	_____	_____
_____ secs	_____ secs	_____ secs	_____ secs

Our results in order:

fastest   slowest

What our results show:

_____

_____

_____

_____

_____

_____

Teachers' notes, page 148

How long are the holidays?

Demonstrates that the child can use a calendar and work from a starting date to an end date.

Using and applying
• *Devises a method to solve problem.*
• *Describes method used.*

Decide which school holiday you want the child to use and fill in the dates on the sheet (before copying). Have a variety of current calendars (or copies of calendar pages) available. Ask the child to complete the sheet, using a calendar for information. Note the child's methods, especially her/his strategies for problem solving.

Note whether the child:
❑ uses a calendar to find information
❑ analyses information correctly

Teacher comments:

from _____   _____   _____

to _____   _____   _____

How many days? _____

How many full weeks? _____

How many Sundays? _____

How did you find out?

Name _____ *Date* _____

Telling the time I

Demonstrates that the child can read 'o'clock' and 'half past' times from an analogue clock and a digital clock, and can mark similar times on a blank analogue or digital clock.

Using and applying
• *Uses maths equipment appropriately.*

Encourage the child to complete the sheet independently. Make sure the child understands what is required; work through an initial example using each type of clock, if necessary.

Note whether the child fills in the gaps correctly:
analogue digital
❑   ❑ o'clock
❑   ❑ ½ past

Note of errors made:
❑ length of hand (analogue)
❑ positioning of digits (digital)

Teacher comments:

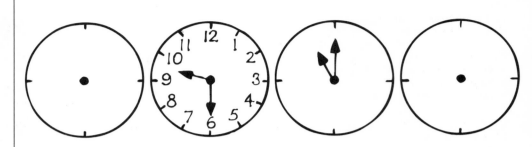

7 o'clock _____ _____ half past 11

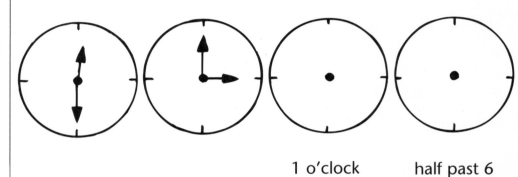

_____ _____ 1 o'clock half past 6

_____

half past 8 p.m.

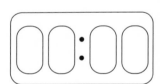
2 o'clock a.m.

_____

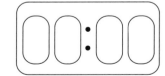
7 o'clock a.m.

1 o'clock p.m.

_____

Teachers' notes, page 149

Name

Date

Telling the time II

Demonstrates that the child can use a digital or analogue clock to work out how long something took.

Using and applying
• *Devises own methods.*
• *Assesses answer to check that it is plausible.*
• *Chooses appropriate units.*

Ask the child to complete the sheet independently, using any appropriate method. At the end, encourage the child to make up her/his own example based on experience, working on the reverse side of the sheet.

Note whether the child can work out amounts of time in:
❑ hours
❑ ½ hours
❑ minutes

Teacher comments:

We went to the hall for PE at 2 o'clock.

We came back at 3 o'clock.

We did PE for _____

I started to read at

I read until

I read for _____

I got up at 8 o'clock.

I went to bed at 7 o'clock.

I was up for _____

I went out to play at

I came in at

I played for _____

I started my packed lunch at ten to 12.

I finished it at quarter past 12.

It took me _____ to eat it.

Name *Date*

Investigating measures

Four measuring challenges:

Demonstrates that the child can choose an appropriate type of measurement, measuring instrument and measuring unit.

Using and applying
- *Justifies choices of equipment.*
- *Devises own methods.*
- *Explains her/his work.*

Prepare the sheet by writing an appropriate measuring challenge at the top of each of the four spaces. The tasks should relate to the four areas of measurement: length, mass, capacity and time. (See Teachers' notes for suggestions.)

Note whether the child can
❏ choose an appropriate measuring instrument
❏ choose appropriate units

Teacher comments:

1	2
3	4

Teachers' notes, page 149

SCOTTISH 5–14 GUIDELINES FOR MATHEMATICS

In this grid, each activity is referenced to the relevant attainment outcome. Within this attainment outcome, the strand and level are identified. The strand is coded to match the level **within which** the child will be working. Please note that completion of a task does not necessarily indicate achievement at that level.

NUMBER, MONEY & ALGEBRA	Range and type of numbers	Money	Add and subtract	Multiply and divide	Round numbers	Fractions, % and ratio	Patterns and sequences	Functions and equations
Numbers	A							
Count it!	B							
Spotty snakes	A							
Guess how many!	A							
Counting up	B							
Do they match?	A							
Hit-a-six	A							
Hop it!	A							
Follow my rule			A/B					
Spot the difference			A					
Make it up I			A/B					
Now you see it...			A					
Mix and match I			A					
Does it add up?			A/B					
Double hit			A/B					B
Does it add up again?			B					
Pictures and words			A					
Up and away			A/B					
How many ways?			B					
Add or take away?			A					B
Making links			A/B	A/B				
The bear facts			A					
Make it, break it			A				B	
Fair shares?				B			B	
Make it up II	A/B							
Sharing out				B				
Mix and match II				B				
Bits and pieces						B		
Thinking about maths I	A		A					
Thinking about maths II	A					B	B	
Before and after	A							
In my head			A/B					
Work it out			B/C					
Many times over				B/C				
Which comes first?	A/B/C							
Making numbers	B/C			B				
Nearest number								
What now?			B/C					
Shopping		A						
Target price		A/B						
Spend £1		B						
Born to shop		B/C						
Fruit corner		B						
In its place							A	
All in order							A	
Round and round							A/B	
Pick a pair							B	
Up and down							A/B	
Number chains			A/B					B

cont...

Information handling

DATA HANDLING	Collect	Organise	Display	Interpret
Sorted!		A		
Dominoes		A		
Sisters and brothers	A		A	
Not this, not that		A		
Double sort		B	B	
Sorting tree		B	B	
Best of three	A/B	A/B	A/B	A/B
Our favourite colour	A/B	A/B	A/B	A/B
What's the difference?	A/B			B
Databases	B/C	B/C	B/C	B/C
Making a graph	B/C	B/C	B/C	B/C

Shape, position and movement

SHAPE AND SPACE	Range of shapes	Position & movement	Symmetry	Angle
Flat shapes	A			
More 2D shapes	A/B			
My first tangram	B			
Short straw, long straw	B			
What's my rule?	A/B			
Is it half?				
3D shape names	A/B			
Does it roll? Does it build?	A			
Making boxes	B			
Boxed in	C			
Symmetrical or not?			B	
Mirror image			B/C	
Fitting together	B			
Looking around	B			
What comes next?				
Where are they?		A		
Spot the right angles				B
Turning		B/C		
Gaps in the hedge		B/C		
Floor robot		B		
Hide and seek		C		

Number, money and measurement

MEASUREMENT	Measure & estimate	Time	Perimeter, formulae, scales
Longer and shorter	A		(see Key Stage 2 book)
Hands and feet	A		
Taller and shorter	A/B		
You and me	B/C		
Estimating	B/C		
Measuring in metres	B		
Covering up	C		
Heavier and lighter	A		
Balancing	A		
My mass	B		
A kilogram	A/B		
Measuring with grams	B/C		
Which holds more?	A		
Fill the pot	A		
More or less than 1 litre	A/B		
Measuring with ml	B/C		
Before and after		A	
What can we do in one minute?		A/B	
Running races		B	
How long are the holidays?		C	
Telling the time I		B	
Telling the time II		C	
Investigating measures	C	C	

NORTHERN IRELAND CURRICULUM FOR MATHEMATICS (KEY STAGE 1)

This grid indicates links between the activities and the relevant sections of the Programmes of Study. For each activity, reference is made to links with 'Processes in mathematics' and the appropriate content areas.

	Processes in mathematics			Number			
NUMBER, MONEY & ALGEBRA	Using mathematics	Communicating mathematically	Mathematical reasoning	Understanding number and number notation	Patterns, relationships and sequences in number	Operations and their applications	Money
Numbers	a	b		a			
Count it!	a			b			
Spotty snakes	a			a			
Guess how many!	a			a/c			
Counting up	a	b		b			
Do they match?	a			a			
Hit-a-six	a			a			
Hop it!		b		a			
Follow my rule	a	b				a	
Spot the difference	d			a		a	
Make it up I		d	a			a/b	
Now you see it...		b	a	a		a	
Mix and match I	a/c					a	
Does it add up?	c	b				a/c	
Double hit	d				c	a	
Does it add up again?	c/d					a/c	
Pictures and words	a	b				c	
Up and away	d	d		a			
How many ways?	d		a/b			a	
Add or take away?	b					a	
Making links	a					a/b	
The bear facts		c/d				a	
Make it, break it	d	d	a		a	c	
Fair shares?	a		a		a	b	
Make it up II	a			d			
Sharing out	d		a			b	
Mix and match II	c	c				b	
Bits and pieces	a	a		d			
Thinking about maths I	a			a		a	
Thinking about maths II	a			d	a	c	
Before and after		a		b			
In my head		b				c	
Work it out		b				c	
Many times over	b					c	
Which comes first?	d			b			
Making numbers	d	b	a	b			
Nearest number		b	a	c			
What now?	a	b				c	
Shopping	a	a/d					a
Target price	b						a
Spend £1	a/b						a
Born to shop	a						a
Fruit corner	a						a
In its place		a/d			a		
All in order	a		a		a		
Round and round	a	b			a		
Pick a pair		d	a		a		
Up and down	a		a		b	c	
Number chains	a/d					c	

cont..

Processes in mathematics — Handling data

DATA HANDLING	Using mathematics	Communicating mathematically	Mathematical reasoning	Collect, represent and interpret data
Sorted!		b/d		a
Dominoes		b/d		a
Sisters and brothers			a	b
Not this, not that	b	b		a
Double sort	b	d	a	a
Sorting tree		d		a
Best of three	d	d		b
Our favourite colour	b	d		b/d
What's the difference?			a	c/d
Databases	d	d		d
Making a graph		d		d

Processes in mathematics — Shape and space

SHAPE AND SPACE	Using mathematics	Communicating mathematically	Mathematical reasoning	Exploration of space	Position, direction & movement
Flat shapes		a		c	
More 2D shapes		a		c	
My first tangram		d		b/c	
Short straw, long straw	d	d		c	
What's my rule?	b	a/d		a	
Is it half?	c	d		b	
3D shape names		a		c	
Does it roll? Does it build?		d	a	a	
Making boxes		a/d		b	
Boxed in	c	d		b	
Symmetrical or not?	a	b		c	
Mirror image	c	b		c	
Fitting together	c	b		b	
Looking around		b/d		b	
What comes next?	b		a	b	
Where are they?		d			a
Spot the right angles			a		b
Turning			a		b
Gaps in the hedge	d		a		b
Floor robot	b/d				c
Hide and seek		d			b

Processes in mathematics — Measures

MEASUREMENT	Using mathematics	Communicating mathematically	Mathematical reasoning	Measures
Longer and shorter	a	b		a
Hands and feet	a	b	a	b
Taller and shorter	a	b/d		c
You and me	a	b		c
Estimating	d	b		c
Measuring in metres	a			c
Covering up	d	b		b
Heavier and lighter	a	b/d		a
Balancing	a	b	b	b
My mass	b	b		c
A kilogram		b	a	c
Measuring with grams	a			c
Which holds more?	c	b		a
Fill the pot		b/d		b
More or less than 1 litre	b		a	c
Measuring with ml	a	b	a	c
Before and after	b	b		a/d
What can we do in one minute?		b		c
Running races	a		a	c
How long are the holidays?		d		d
Telling the time I	a			e
Telling the time II	c			e
Investigating measures	a	b		c